New English, New Imperatives

EDITED BY HENRY B. MALONEY
University of Detroit

NATIONAL COUNCIL OF TEACHERS OF ENGLISH
508 South Sixth Street/Champaign, Illinois 61820

CONSULTANT READERS FOR THIS MANUSCRIPT Zora M. Rashkis, Grey Culbreth Junior High School, Chapel Hill, North Carolina/ George F. Nemetz, State of California Department of Education, Sacramento/ NCTE COMMITTEE ON PUBLICATIONS Robert F. Hogan, NCTE Executive Secretary, Chairman/ Robert Dykstra, University of Minnesota/ Walker Gibson, University of Massachusetts, Amherst/ Mildred E. Webster, St. Joseph Senior High School, Michigan/ Eugene C. Ross, NCTE Director of Publications/EDITORIAL SERVICES Robyn Grant D'Alba, NCTE Headquarters/BOOK DESIGN Norma Phillips Meyers, NCTE Headquarters

Library of Congress Catalog Card Number LC 78-146491
ISBN 0-8141-0385-5
NCTE Stock Number 03855

Contents

Preface

This is a read-and-do book.

It is dedicated to and aimed at secondary English departments that have failed to engage in any comprehensive self-evaluation since 1966.* My hope is that the nine papers included in this book will help those English departments to examine their programs critically and encourage them to take action that will bring about changes appropriate to their schools and their students' needs. To attempt to gain safe and salubrious passage through the seventies with an English program that neglects to touch students or neglects to engage the seventies themselves is folly of a dangerous sort.

The papers gathered here were presented at the 1969 Spring Institutes for chairmen of high school English departments and supervisors. These institutes, which focused on the theme, "New English, New Imperatives," were held in Springfield (Massachusetts), St. Louis, Santa Barbara, and Richmond. It would be delightful to review each institute in detail since the rearview mirror has rose-tinted glass in this instance. Thanks to the able speakers;

---

* This cutoff date is suggested by the Anglo-American Conference at Dartmouth and the development of an ungraded, phase-elective program at Trenton (Michigan) High School. Both of these events occurred in the summer of 1966. Both have pointed out several ways in which high school English programs can be strengthened to deal with the problems and stresses of the new decade.

to the diligence of the four local chairmen—Richard Ulin, Maxine Delmare, Gretchen Wheelwright, and Frances Wimer; and to the adroit handling of large and small problems by G. Rodney Morisset, an assistant executive secretary of NCTE, the institutes proved to be a stimulating cognitive and affective experience. But affectionate reminiscence will hardly help the purpose of this book, so I will mention only two matters that ought to be documented.

The four themes of the institutes were the Dartmouth Conference, Secondary English Curriculums, Organization of High School English Departments, and New Imperatives in the Teaching of English. Different groups of speakers addressed these topics at each of the four sites. The original plan for this book called for inclusion of the four papers on the Dartmouth Conference along with the four on New Imperatives, but certain developments forced a deviation from this plan. First, important new directions and new imperatives were described in three papers that were not given during the New Imperatives part of the program. Because they are pertinent to the goals of assessment and change, these three papers have been included here. As a consequence, other presentations do not appear in the collection. Finally, a bit of a communication breakdown between the Americans and the English resulted in Geoffrey Summerfield's speaking at two institutes. He is therefore represented by two papers in this book. Thus, the book includes nine papers, one more than the initial blueprint called for.

One of the aims of the institutes was to see how the twenty-three recommendations for high school departments of English were faring.* Since the recommendations had been put into final form at a conference in Cleveland nearly five years earlier, it seemed appropriate to assess their durability as guidelines and to determine to what extent they were being implemented. A statistical analysis on a recommendation by recommendation basis seemed too time consuming and too formal for the tone of the institutes. As an alternative, the four leaders at each institute were advised to invite their groups to talk about those recommendations that were still matters of concern to them. Recorders were assigned to report the highlights of each discussion back to the total group.

---

* *High School Departments of English: Their Organization, Administration, and Supervision.* Champaign, Illinois: National Council of Teachers of English, 1965.

Their reports were taped, and the substance of the comments that follow was drawn from an audit of the sixteen taped reports.

A few other prefatory remarks merit mention. Each small group had only about forty-five minutes in which to comment on the twenty-three proposals. In addition, although the discussion leaders in each city were given the same general briefing regarding this part of the institute, no serious effort was made to give identical directions at each site. Indeed, the different kinds of feedback received from the four recorders in each city suggested that (1) some discussion leaders interpreted their charge to keep the discussions interesting as a mandate to stay on the periphery of the recommendations, (2) some English teachers like the apparent precision that a survey affords, and (3) the term *highlights* means different things to different people. Interestingly, the suggestion that we chuck all twenty-three recommendations was not considered a highlight and consequently did not get a hearing at a plenary session. In spite of these shortcomings in collecting data scientifically, I maintain that the summary which follows is a fairly representative statement that indicates which recommendations remain matters of concern.

Generally, the institute participants agreed with the recommendations and felt that identifying them and compiling them had helped bring about implementation in their departments. The areas of major concern centered around four recommendations:

Recommendation No. 6: The department chairman should work out basic agreements about content and sequence with (1) members of his department, (2) department chairmen of other high schools in the district, and (3) those responsible for the English program at levels above and below the high school.

Recommendation No. 10: The English department chairman should play a major role in recruiting and selecting English teachers.

Recommendation No. 13: Each chairman should teach at least one class, but for each five teachers or major fraction thereof, he should be released one period—in addition to his regular preparation period—for duties as English department chairman.

Recommendation No. 15: Chairmen should encourage the English faculty to cooperate with local teacher education institutions in providing varied and necessary field experiences for student teachers.

One can see at once that a close relationship exists between Recommendation No. 13 and the others. The department chairman who is overburdened and short of time is not likely to be recruiting teachers, initiating articulation meetings, or working closely with teacher education institutions.

Unfortunately, this situation seems to prevail in many high schools. The recorders indicated that department chairmen are in most instances not getting the time for administrative responsibilities which was proposed in Recommendation No. 13. Furthermore, because the time available to them is often consumed by routine clerical chores that relate to their own schools, they inevitably must give a low priority to important outside concerns, since, in the hierarchy of values, other schools are entitled to only the time that is left after the home school is served.

Some chairmen do have an opportunity to interview and screen prospective members of their departments. Too many, however, must accept and work with new staff members that have been selected without their involvement. Since the Dartmouth Conference and other developments in English during the past five years have brought about significant changes in the delineation of the ideal English teacher, the department chairmen believed that it was imperative that they take part in hiring English teachers if their departments were to be strong and prepared to teach today's English.

Finally, there were major concerns that discussions with teacher training institutions were too much of a one-way street. The chairmen wanted more cooperation from the colleges. Some thought that the colleges ought to make the minimum requirements for student teachers more rigorous; others believed that faculty members in teacher training ought to become more familiar with what goes on in high school classrooms. There were also suggestions that methods of compensating cooperating teachers be reviewed.

The other recommendations were touched on, but interest in them seemed to be contingent upon local conditions.

For a few English departments the observations and recommendations in these nine papers will undoubtedly seem out of date already. (One of the problems of the institutes was that of trying to communicate with an audience that included various degrees of sophistication about the New English. In Santa Barbara, for example, one ad hoc group chose to spend a large block of time drafting a rationale for abolishing letter grades. Not everyone was prepared to move this far personally or as the representative of a school with a conservative or moderate philosophy.) But to those who have not engaged in self-examination since 1966, the ideas here are likely to seem fresh, perhaps even dangerously far out.

In order to precipitate discussion leading to self-assessment and change, thirty-five provocative statements from the nine papers have been gathered in a section called "Points for Discussion." They appear at the end of the book. Two other ingredients from the institutes would be most helpful in generating concern about the status quo:

A *description of the Trenton High School ungraded, phase-elective English program*. One of the publications included in the institute packets was a detailed description of Trenton's APEX curriculum. The basic plan is flexible enough to be used in a variety of school situations. It is available at a cost of $2.00 per copy from Donald Weise, Chairman, English Department, Trenton High School, 2601 Charlton Road, Trenton, Michigan 48183.

The two BBC films on improvised drama mentioned in Albert Marckwardt's paper. Either of these, which run for about twenty-five minutes each, would be adequate.

Why must English programs change? This book should provide many answers to that question. Still another reason for change, however, was given in an editorial by Norman Cousins in the August 29, 1964 issue of *Saturday Review*. It is even more urgent today than it was when it was written.

Hope today—and it may be the only hope— resides in the world-wide emergence of the articulate and communicating citizen.

I would add to that statement—and the citizen who is able to rekindle his sense of outrage, which is also a form of communication.

Henry B. Maloney
Director, 1969 Spring Institutes
University of Detroit

1

Dartmouth and After:
Issues in English Language Teaching

As I understand the organization of this spring's series of institutes, we are to focus upon the theme of "New English, New Imperatives," using the Dartmouth Conference as a point of departure. That there are new imperatives, I readily concede, and I shall try to explore some of them in the course of my discussion. Whether there is a new English, in the sense that we have a new mathematics or a new science, seems to me to be a somewhat more dubious proposition. If it needs to be considered at all, it can conveniently be deferred until somewhat later. And even though the Dartmouth Conference has been pinpointed for us as a *terminus a quo*, we must realize that it did not spring forth

Albert H. Marckwardt/Princeton University/Presented at the Richmond Institute

fully caparisoned, either from the brain of Jove or the coffers of the Carnegie Corporation. It had a background peculiarly its own, and it will be helpful, I believe, if we take a little time to trace it.

Since one must begin somewhere in the account of a developmental process, I shall choose as a starting point the Basic Issues Conference of 1958. This series of meetings was notable for three innovations in the English-teaching climate of the late 1950s. First, and possibly most important, it marked the beginning of the now very strong cooperation between the Modern Language Association and the National Council of Teachers of English on matters pertaining to the teaching of English and to the profession responsible for it. I have told this story elsewhere, in some detail, and shall not repeat the account of the steps leading to it. The important point is that two powerful organizations, hitherto somewhat suspicious of each other's motives, each of them zealous in guarding what it considered to be its legitimate areas, were able to work together with a minimum of friction and a considerable amount of mutual benefit. It is still too early, perhaps, to realize fully the impact of the cooperative impulse which was generated here, but I can say with confidence that I know of nothing like it in any other subject-matter field over the entire educational spectrum.

The second point about the Basic Issues Conference which must be understood is that neither the discussions nor the report emanating from it offered solutions to the then-current problems. It attempted, instead, to formulate and clarify the educational issues which lay beneath them, to pose them in what the participants hoped would be an open-minded and neutral fashion, thus stimulating a number of serious endeavors to find the answers. As an illustration of what I mean here, let me cite just one of the thirty-five basic issues which comprised the final report: "Can basic programs in English be devised that are sequential and cumulative from the kindergarten through the graduate school?" Here, as in every other instance, the issue was posed in the form of a question, but it was also followed by a commentary accounting for its inclusion. Since this particular issue will have some import for us later on, it is worth quoting at least part of the comment which accompanied it. "This issue seems crucial to this entire document," wrote the conferees, "and to any serious approach to the problem.

Unless we can find an answer to it, we must resign ourselves to an unhappy future in which the present curricular disorder persists and the whole liberal discipline of English continues to disintegrate and lose its character."

Despite these strenuous efforts at neutrality, the conference was operating in a climate of post-Sputnik shock, and accordingly it is not surprising to find that the issues posed in its report tended to be content-centered. Given the circumstances, I do not find this at all surprising or unnatural. In fact, I am inclined to feel that content was the one basis upon which the Modern Language Association and the NCTE could have arrived at some mutual understanding, and in the light of all that has happened since, I am grateful that the bridge was built.

From 1962 on, with the development of the Curriculum Study Centers and the NDEA Institutes, the sphere of cooperation widened perceptibly. Lines of communication between the scholars in the academic departments and the professional educators were established, as were those with the teachers in the schools. A medievalist with a doctorate from an Ivy League university suddenly found himself teamed with a specialist in English education, in charge of developing a total curriculum for grades K-13 for an entire midwestern state. Although the example is a bit extreme, it is typical of the spirit that was generated. The core of these efforts was still primarily content, especially at the outset, but by this time tempered with a realistic sense of what was achievable, based upon direct contact with the schools.

Thus far the enlarged sphere of cooperation was almost wholly confined to this country. The initial recognition that there might be some advantage in comparing our practices and problems in connection with the teaching of English with those of other English-speaking nations came with the organization of an International Conference on the Teaching of English, cosponsored by the NCTE and by the National Association for the Teaching of English, its British counterpart, only a few years old at the time. This international conference, involving Canadians as well as members of the profession from the United States and the United Kingdom, was held in connection with the 1965 annual meeting of the NCTE, which took place in Boston. There were forty-four participants in all, about equally divided among the three participating countries. The stated purpose of the conference was "to compare and contrast the ends and means of instruction in our common language."

In terms of the time that was available for discussion, the conference was generally successful. A number of topics had been assigned to teams of two or three, one person from this country and a British or Canadian counterpart or both. These introductory papers were read before the entire conference and were then taken up both in plenary sessions and in small group discussions. This served to bring into the open differing points of view, but in the short space of three days, there was insufficient opportunity to arrive at an exploration of issues, to say nothing of their resolution. What was demonstrated here, however, was the potential value of an international dialogue, and the degree to which we, on the two sides of the Atlantic, were facing similar problems and concerns, that we indeed had *A Common Purpose*, the title given to the published proceedings.

Even before this conference had taken place, plans for a more extended meeting were under way, having been formulated by a small committee which met in England the preceding month. What we wanted was time, time for study and reflection as well as for discussion. Our idea was to involve approximately forty-five to fifty persons, the bulk of the representation to be divided about equally from Britain and the United States, but with due regard for a Canadian voice as well. We hoped also that all levels of education and all shades of professional opinion might be included. After some effort, the project was funded by the Carnegie Corporation, and a month-long meeting was held on the Dartmouth campus in late August and early September 1966. I shall be honest and admit that not every one of our hopes was fully realized, but many of them were, and the effect of this month of close contact and discussion upon the contingent from the United States was electrifying. For the next six months at least, whenever two Dartmouth participants met, it seemed as if they could talk of nothing else, sometimes to the decided annoyance of whoever else happened to be present. We did feel that the British contingent was short in representation from the older British universities; Oxbridge was represented by only one professor of literature. On the other hand, we from the

United States had little to match the brilliant group of young classroom teachers from the secondary schools in the British contingent —most of whom, incidentally, have since moved out of the secondary-school classrooms they then occupied.

The Dartmouth Conference itself resulted in some striking points of agreement and some unlooked for points of disagreement. Among the former was a profound opposition to tracking or streaming, that is to say ability grouping, as it operated in both countries— and I hasten to say that it operates in a somewhat different manner. In addition, there was a strong disposition to question the way in which testing and examination policies operated. It was the consensus of the conference that these were a hindrance rather than a help to the educational process, both in their American and in their British guise, and I must point out that we had a then member of the staff of the Educational Testing Service with us part of the time as a consultant.

I have treated the points of disagreement elsewhere in some detail, and I shall do little more here than merely to mention them. There was virtually no disposition on the part of the British contingent to accept our view that one part, at least, of the function of teaching English literature was to transmit the national cultural heritage to the younger generation. On this point our only ally among the British was one of Her Majesty's Inspectors who was a Welshman and who had Wales for his territory. To the English it appeared that our phrase, "transmitting the cultural heritage," was a deftly concealed euphemism for freezing into the educational system a whole set of middle-class values and mores sadly in need of change. The idea of a carefully planned and sequenced curriculum, one of the fundamental hypotheses of the Basic Issues Conference report, caused the British to react with something little short of absolute horror. As I have put it on another occasion, they obviously prefer flying by the seat of their trousers to using a navigational chart. Nor did they share our concern for an emphasis upon the prestige dialect of English for speakers of the nonstandard language. Since I shall have more to say about this point later on, I shall not enlarge upon it now. All that I want to say here is that there was disagreement.

Despite these differences, and they were by no means trivial, the exciting thing that did emerge from the conference was the concept of English as consisting principally of experience and involvement. For this I must credit the British for the major share of the responsibility, although it was evident that some of the Americans were already thinking along the same lines, notably Benjamin DeMott and James Moffett.

When I speak of experience, however, I must make it clear that this is by no means a return to the pale and mistaken application of John Dewey's educational philosophy which got written into the so-called *experience curriculum* of the mid-1930s. I mention this because there has been some misunderstanding and some misinterpretation of the Dartmouth Conference on this point. We are not talking here about practicing telephone conversations or writing or replying to party invitations on the ground that these are activities which adults do engage in, and if we are to give the students practice in language it may as well be done in terms of such activities. This earlier approach emphasized and utilized an anticipation of adult experiences, some of them trivial, others unrealistically conceived, and some open to both charges.

What the conference meant by experience was the sharing of experience, the use of language by man to make that experience real to himself. To quote John Dixon, author of *Growth through English,* one of the book-length reports on the conference, "Recalling experience, getting it clear, giving it shape and making connections, speculating and building theories, celebrating (or exorcizing) particular moments of our lives—these are some of the broad purposes that language serves and enables." And just as life, either real or imagined, furnishes the only viable basis for experience, so literature must be chosen, measured, and utilized in terms of response. In short, one does not learn literature, one responds to it, experiences or feels it—gets hooked by it, to use Daniel Fader's phrase. One rarely says anything important in the real sense in talk or in writing unless it is something that he feels, that he is truly motivated to express.

In this sense, the approach and philosophy of the Dartmouth Conference is not fundamentally different from that of the Living Theater, as it was set forth in an article by Professor Daniel Selzer in the *Harvard Alumni Bulletin.* One could almost paraphrase the sentence I am going to quote and apply it to the English-teaching situation.

> As a teacher concerned with new developments in drama as well as with new developments in the past, I am convinced that the radical importance of the Living Theater is undeniable, that any approach to performance in the future must necessarily be influenced by it, and that the group's potential for involving an audience in dramatic action forces one to reconsider some of the most fundamental theories relating to the origins and practice of the drama.

To repeat, the key words here are *experience* and *involvement*. Another one, which has found its way into a National Council publication is *response,* response to literature.

Let me make it clear that there are difficulties here, chiefly in setting up situations in which involvement or response occurs, and second in drawing from the pupils the best efforts of which they are capable. These same problems occur also in connection with the Living Theater. Let me quote again some sentences from Selzer's article: "Long stretches of the four productions were by no means so vivid. I was bored some of the time and I know that many other spectators—participants?—were bored perhaps more than I was, or at different times." But significantly, "Some were more involved than I." And again, "You cannot demand from every individual the sort of confrontation demanded every moment by members of this company; or at least, if you demand it, you must expect some people to retain their right . . . to say no." And finally, "During the latter moments, when one attends to the play in which one is a silent actor, much that the Living Theater does can seem childish, self-indulgent, and silly." These negative reactions as well as the positive are not unlike those which might well arise from attempts to apply the Dartmouth philosophy to the English classroom. Admittedly this is a real challenge to the teacher.

In essence, this is what occurred at the Dartmouth Conference. I am quite certain that I can anticipate the next question: So you met and talked and worked yourselves up into a state of excitement. What happens now? From the very outset we tried to build some follow-up into the plans for the conference. Not all of them have been realized, but many of them have. I shall mention a number of them briefly.

Two books setting forth the conclusions and the progress of the argument at the conference have been published. One has already been mentioned: *Growth through English* by John Dixon; the second is *The Uses of English* by Herbert J. Muller. Mr. Dixon's book was intended for members of the English-teaching profession, Mr. Muller's for the general public. In addition, a series of six monographs representing the workpapers and specific conclusions of the various study groups has appeared.

As a direct outgrowth of the conference an international steering committee was organized. The principal function of this body, which meets once a year, is to do whatever is possible in the way of implementing the decisions of the group which met at Dartmouth. This committee has been responsible for making available in the United States films of the skillful use of drama in classrooms in Britain.[1] It is planning an international anthology of children's writing. It attempted, unsuccessfully, to fund an investigation of testing practices in Britain and the United States. It is currently undertaking an investigation of the teaching of the native language and literature in a number of western European countries on the assumption that the English-speaking countries might have something to learn from nations like Holland, Norway, and West Germany.

There is every reason to believe that the discussions at Dartmouth had an influence on *Guidelines for the Preparation of Teachers of English,* published by NCTE, and it is not unreasonable to assume that they played a significant role in stimulating and influencing the Squire-Applebee study of classroom practices in secondary schools in Great Britain.[2] A Schools/Universities Conference on the teaching of English literature was held in England in September 1968. It is fair to say that we have been more successful in our attempts to implement the results of the Dartmouth Conference than we were a decade ago with the Basic Issues Conference.

My own field of specialization is the English language, and you may be wondering where this fits into the general Dartmouth picture. Actually, several matters of linguistic interest were explored with our British colleagues. The first of these dealt with usage, with particular reference to the way in which linguistic standards and attitudes develop. There were few real disagreements on this score. In my own initial paper I attempted to disarm and mollify my literary colleagues, who sometimes feel that the linguists' commitment to a descriptive approach is shortsighted and even fraught with some danger. I attempted to do this by demonstrating that the descriptivism of the linguists was often misunderstood, by pointing out that the English language in our society was far too complex to admit of a monolithic standard, and that we must make due allowance for attitude toward language as well as actual usage. The paper seemed to have served these purposes fairly well; at least it avoided the customary hassle between linguists and literary scholars on this score.

I was speaking, of course, only in terms of the situation in the United States; that in Britain is somewhat different. Despite the post-world war democratization and the broadening of the educational base, there is still a greater degree of social stratification in Britain than there is here. Consequently there is a greater willingness on the part of the British to admit that class differences in language do exist; there is less nervousness and anxiety about these differences, less hypocrisy about what constitutes the standard. Although standard British use is possibly more easily defined, our more generalized prestige dialect has the advantage of giving us a greater number of alternatives to choose from. It is true also that within the British culture, the teacher, and particularly the English teacher, is not looked upon as the supreme arbiter of the standard to the extent that he is with us.

On this latter point it is still of some interest to read what an Englishman, Professor Alan S. C. Ross of the University of Birmingham (England), wrote in 1956:

> In England today—just as much as in the England of many years ago—the question "Can a non-U[pper class] speaker become a U-speaker?" is one noticeably of paramount importance for many Englishmen (and for some of their wives). The answer is that an adult can never attain complete success . . . Under these circumstances, efforts to change voice are surely better abandoned . . . But, in fact, they continue in full force and in all strata of society. On the whole, the effect is deleterious. Thus, to take only one example: in village schools, any natural dialect that is still left to the children will have superimposed upon it the language of the primary school-teacher (a class of people entirely non-U) so that

the children leave school speaking a mixture which has nothing to recommend it.[3]

Note that there are two or three attitudes here which would not be generally shared in the United States: first, that it is better to leave the natural dialect of the children untouched than to impose a mixture upon them; second, that the imposition of a mixture is the most that can be achieved in any event; and finally, that the language of the schoolteacher is scarcely appropriate to serve as a model—definitely non-U, so to speak.

Despite these differences in attitude, I believe it fair to say that there was general agreement between British and Americans that our methods of surveying the language in order to determine what is acceptable and standard are in need of considerable refinement. We have not recognized sufficiently that there are many styles, or registers as the British call them, suitable to different kinds of communications situations, each with its own standard or prestige behavior. We have not studied sufficiently the structural differences between the spoken and written forms of the language and are too much inclined to rely upon general impression with respect to these matters. As an illustration of this, I can point to a doctoral dissertation of a few years ago which individually compared the spoken and written language of some twenty authors and turned up the surprising information that the corpus of spoken English contained a higher proportion of subordinate clauses. There are two bodies of collected material, one each in Britain and America, which would bear investigation. One of these is the corpus of one million running words collected by Professor W. Nelson Francis of Brown University; the other, a body of material of comparable extent in the hands of Professor Randolph Quirk of the University of London. Both sets of materials have been subjected to some analysis; what we need now is a clearly presented report on usage easily accessible to and understandable by classroom teachers.

As might have been expected, the Dartmouth Conference brought to light some differences between the Americans and the British in their attitude toward the potential usefulness of linguistics in the classroom situation. The linguists have long claimed that it is impossible, or at least scarcely feasible, for the classroom teacher to hope to deal with language problems effectively without some knowledge of the science of language. In both countries these claims have given rise to a certain amount of skepticism, but not always for the same reasons. For one thing, there are fewer so-called schools of linguistics in Britain, where the general approach to linguistic study might be characterized as neo-Firthian, that is to say the general approach of J. R. Firth with some minor modifications. In this country the competing claims of the structuralists, the tagmemicists, the generative-transformationalists, and now the stratificationalists, have understandably led English teachers to a state of confusion and to a readiness to wash their hands of the whole thing.

Moreover, there has been nothing in Britain at all comparable to the recent outpour of linguistically-oriented language teaching materials which we have had in the United States, in large part at least as a result of the work done by the government-supported curriculum study centers. It almost seems as if every American publisher now feels that he must have his captive linguist, complete with beard and computer. In general there is nothing wrong with this except the irony that for years it was impossible to get even a single publisher to venture enough risk capital to put one linguistically based book on the market. The American situation does pose a problem, however. No textbook or series of textbooks is capable of solving a teaching problem by itself, especially when a new or different approach underlies it. We are all aware of the difficulties this has posed in connection with the teaching of mathematics. English is no different. Linguistically based textbooks will succeed only if we take the trouble to acquaint teachers with the principles upon which they are based and train them in their use. This takes more than a one-day workshop with casual attention to classroom tricks or devices. It requires a totally different way of looking at language which cannot be communicated in a once-over-lightly fashion.

On the other hand, if we are ahead of the British in the matter of linguistically oriented teaching materials, we must give them credit for having surpassed us in the solidly based linguistic research they have done on the language of children. There are a number of major projects going on there, financed in part by the

Nuffield Foundation and in part by the Schools Council. But again there is the usual gap between what the research teams are finding out and its application to classroom practices.

The most urgent problem facing both countries is really sociolinguistic, having to do with the language of the so-called disadvantaged, and in each country there is a core question centering about ethnic minorities. Britain is acquiring its concentration of West Indian migrants, and there are other newcomers as well who are experiencing language difficulties. In the United States it is somewhat more complex, in that we must deal with the black pupils, many but not all of whom represent recent migration from the South; the Puerto Ricans who, like the blacks are clustered in our urban centers but for whom English is a foreign language despite their American citizenship; and the American Indians, who also present a foreign-language problem but who are not clustered in urban centers. All of these are urgent matters; each requires a somewhat different treatment.

In this area the problems have been increasing at an accelerated pace and circumstances have forced us to go considerably beyond the attention which the Dartmouth Conference gave to the matter and the conclusions which were arrived at there. Almost all of the issues were anticipated, to be sure, but during the last two years feelings about some of them have mounted and unfortunately the discussions have not always been rational and cool.

The first point of disagreement is the extent to which habitual use of or commitment to a nonstandard dialect represents linguistic deprivation. This is the view taken by such psychologists as Carl Bereiter in the United States and such sociologists as Basil Bernstein in England. Bereiter believes, and I quote from his chapter in the NCTE Task Force report, that "by the time they are five years old, disadvantaged children of almost every kind are typically one to two years retarded in language development. This is supported by virtually any index of language development one cares to look at." I shall have more to say about these indices later on. Similarly, Bernstein has characterized the language of British working-class children as a "restricted code," in contrast to that of middle-class children, which he speaks of as an "elaborated code." In both instances, the assumption seems to be that the culturally disadvantaged haven't any words to work with in the first place, and any structures to put them in, in the second.

There has been vigorous opposition to these views on the part of some linguists, notably those who have made a specialty of the study of dialects and of creolized languages. This opposition takes the form of two counter-arguments. The first is that Bereiter and his fellow psychologists simply have not mastered the art of eliciting language from their youthful subjects. They tend to place the child in what he interprets as an alien and a threatening situation. There the youngster assumes a defensive posture and refuses to talk freely. It is then assumed from his lack of response that he has nothing to say and no language to say it with. William Labov, undoubtedly the most able of the younger generation of linguistic geographers and students of dialect, asserts, "Such behavior can be produced at will in any group of children and can be altered by changing the relevant socio-linguistic variables."

The second difficulty has arisen from the failure of the psychologists and often the professional educators to understand that nonstandard dialects, whether of the urban or the Appalachian variety, have their own structure which, though it may at times fail to signal some of the distinctions customary in standard English, at other times will contain subtleties which the standard language ignores or which the speaker of standard English is not aware of. William Stewart, who has worked extensively with dialects in Washington, D.C., has pointed out for example that there is a distinction between *He sick* and *He be sick,* the first indicating a temporary or momentary state and the second a habitual or lasting condition. Elsewhere he has shown that the dialect he has been working with, "does not normally inflect the verb in any way to show the difference between the simple present and the preterit, e.g., *I see it* . . . can mean either 'I see it,' or 'I saw it.'" On the other hand, in the same dialect there is not only the simple perfect construction *I seen it* (I have seen it) but also a completive perfect, *I been seen it,* with primary stress on *been,* regularly used in the sense of *I have already seen it some time ago.* At the same time, though the simple present and the preterit are identical in their affirmative form, the fact that they exist as separate grammatical categories is indicated by the fact that the two are negated differently: *I don't see it* for the present and *I ain't see it* (i.e. I didn't see it) for the past.

In short, nonstandard grammar has its own logic and its own system, and in fact so does each nonstandard dialect, and as logic and as system there is no reason to consider them either better or worse than the logic and system of the prestige dialect. If we are in a mood to pick flaws, let me point to the mess which standard English has made of the reflexive pronoun, with half of the paradigm based upon the genitive form of the pronoun plus *self* (myself, yourself), and the other half formed with the object pronoun plus *self* (himself, themselves). Let me point as well to the equally irrational jumble where *my* adds *n* to form the absolute *mine*, where *your* adds *s* to form its absolute, and where with the pronoun *his* the two forms are not distinguished. Let me point to the fact that we have no negative form for *used to* or for *ought* with which we can be wholly comfortable. The simple fact is that no dialect of English presents us with a flawless grammatical system; the superiority of the prestige dialect we call standard English derives not from internal but from external social factors.

The principle I have just enunciated was well known to all of us at the Dartmouth Conference, at least to the eight or nine linguists there. What has occurred since that time has been a considerable amount of investigation into urban dialects all over the country; in New York, Chicago, Philadelphia, Pittsburgh, Washington, Detroit—to name just a few. I shall deal a little later with the uses to which these investigations are being put. My principal concern at this time is to give a *coup de grace* to the traditional view of nonstandard English, long held by many public school teachers and professional educators, that it is an illogical form of speech, and that when children are taught the standard forms, they are also being taught to think logically. This is a bit of old folklore which dies hard and which, in its time, has assumed many guises. It was the chief argument employed by the teachers of Greek during the Renaissance to encourage the study of that language. Even today, if you lurk about the corridors of a meeting of the American Association of Teachers of French, you will hear it repeated with respect to that language, but in these instances it is not English dialects which are being smeared by the comparison, but the entire English language, lock, stock, and barrel.

Even before the Dartmouth Conference, there had been some uncertainty about the extent to which the standard language was to figure in our teaching aims. Was it to be imposed upon the student as a replacement for his native dialect, or was he to be left with a functional bi-dialectalism? For the most part, the climate of opinion had favored the latter, but at Dartmouth and since there have been a few who have gone so far as to insist that we have no right at all to tamper with a pupil's natural speech, and that what we should be doing is to reform the public insistence upon a single standard in the direction of a greater tolerance. Professors James Sledd and Wayne O'Neill have been particularly emphatic in their advocacy of this point of view. It was also true that at Dartmouth the British contingent was content to assume a laissez-faire principle with respect to the speech of the pupils—much less so with their writing, though even here there was far greater concern with the sincerity and immediacy of what they wrote than with the style in which they wrote it.

Two observations may be made in this connection. Admittedly a greater linguistic tolerance is a desirable goal, but it will take decades if not generations to achieve; and meanwhile there is a host of practical problems to be met in connection with employment opportunities for speakers of nonstandard English. These can scarcely be brushed aside. As far as the British attitude is concerned, I was told some months after the conference by a member of the British contingent that they had no idea of the breadth of the gap which separated many of the urban dialects from the standard language, and had they known the actual state of affairs, their attitudes might have been quite different.

Closely connected with all of this is the issue of inherent racism in the language we use. The most extensive expression of this which I have encountered appeared in an article by Ossie Davis in the *American Teacher* for April 1967. It is entitled "The English Language Is My Enemy," and makes its point chiefly by indicating the number of synonyms for the word *whiteness* in Roget's *Thesaurus* which have a favorable connotation, and those for the word *black-*

ness which are pejorative in character. It was convenient for the author of course not to mention such a compound as *white-livered,* meaning deficient in vigor and courage, or the halo of glory which surrounds the Black Prince and the Black Watch. Despite this quibble, however, and some convenient omissions in the author's use of statistics, it must be confessed that he has a point: that in this culture *white* and *whiteness* are ameliorative more often than pejorative, and that the opposite is true for *black* and *blackness.*

The extent to which this reflects overt or conscious racism is quite another matter. I find it a little difficult to level this charge at the seventh-century *Beowulf* poet because he described the lair of Grendel's dam in terms of murkiness and blackness. And I note as well that the figurative association of fierceness, terror, and wickedness with the adjective *black* goes back to the fourteenth century, and with the verb to the early fifteenth; that is to say, long before the race problem assumed its peculiar American dimension.

Much as I wish that something might be done about this, I don't quite know what positive measures can be taken. These aspects of language change slowly, and conscious attempts at alteration seem to have little effect except to create a series of partial taboos. Something can be done in the way of sensitivity training, making people aware of what seems calculated to produce hurt feelings, but beyond that I fear the going will be slow.

The extremely sensitive are also inclined to perceive racist and establishment overtones in the use of the term *standard* for the prestige dialect, but this arises in part from a misunderstanding of the linguist's use of the term, which is intended to be wholly neutral. He needs some label for that form of the language which has acquired its prestige from the fact that, as C. C. Fries once said, it is the language of those who are carrying on the affairs of the English-speaking people. As evidence of the caution exercised by linguists on this point and of their desire to avoid pejorative overtones, I need only to point to the replacement of the terms *vulgar* and *illiterate* by *substandard,* and the more recent tendency toward the use of *nonstandard.* Any linguist will readily admit that as the power structure shifts, the standard will shift along with it. This occurred in thirteenth-century England, again in sixteenth-century England. It is happening with some of our southern dialects now, and similar changes are undoubtedly in the offing both in Britain and in our northern urban centers. As I have indicated before, the problem here is one of improving our techniques of describing usage more fully and with greater accuracy than we have been able to up to this time.

Within the past few years some confusion has arisen over the supposed similarity between teaching standard English as a second dialect and teaching English—or any other language—as a second or foreign language. On the average of once every three or four months a news release appears, reporting that Teacher X, operating in this or that city, has proceeded to teach standard English to her urban or rural disadvantaged just as if she were teaching them another language. The account invariably reads as if this were a totally new discovery, and of course extraordinary success is claimed for the technique.

The fact is that there are certain similarities in the two situations, but at the same time there are important differences. I feel impelled to take these up in some detail, primarily so that the teacher, curriculum consultant, or administrator will not fall an easy prey to the first earnest publisher's representative or glib electronics salesman who crosses his path. Let us look first at the differences. The speaker of nonstandard English, especially if he lives in an urban environment, is surrounded, assailed on every side by the prestige dialect. He hears it on the radio, the television, the film sound track, and from a considerable number of the persons he encounters in his daily life. This is true of the foreign-language learner only if he learns the language in the country where it is spoken natively. It is not true of the pupil learning French, German, or Spanish in the average school in the United States.

As a consequence of his being in a standard English environment for part of the time, at any rate, the speaker of a nonstandard dialect is likely to have a considerable receptive acquaintance with the standard language, especially with the vocabulary. The teaching problem with such a person, therefore, is to extend the receptive command and to convert it into productive ability. Again this is quite different from the case of the foreign-language student, who begins with no receptive experience whatsoever. He does not comprehend what he hears and cannot understand what he reads.

Moreover, the productive command of the speaker of nonstandard will include some features of the standard dialect. As I pointed out some time ago, he finds that there is nothing wrong with his negation of *I see it* in the present tense, namely *I don't see it,* but runs into difficulty with both the statement and negation in the past, where his *I see it* and *I ain't see it* run counter to the standard forms *I saw it* and *I didn't see it.*

This does suggest the basic similarity between foreign language and standard dialect learning. What is required in both instances is an inventory of the features to be mastered. In both instances, the way in which to compile this inventory is to compare the structure of the language or the dialect which the learner normally employs with the structure of the language to be taught, in order to get at the points of difference, whether they be in phonology, syntax, or lexicon. The teaching emphasis, in both cases, must be placed on the points which differ. Those which are the same can be taken for granted as not requiring any particular attention. For the others, many of the same devices, pattern drill, laboratory exercises, etc., can be employed as an aid in establishing the desired habits. Overuse of these devices or too mechanical a resort to them may have the same pitfalls in either native or foreign language instruction. Nevertheless, to equate the two absolutely is a mistake, both pedagogically and psychologically.

A final question which always arises in connection with language teaching, whether it be native or foreign, is that of the place of linguistics in the training of teachers and its potential application in the classroom. The Dartmouth Conference did little to produce any positive convictions on these matters. Those who came to the conference believing that linguistics has a role here, and this included both British and Americans, came away with that belief unshaken, as the last page of *Language and Language Learning* [4] clearly indicates. Those who doubted its value continued to doubt. Fortunately the linguists at the conference were a fairly unabrasive lot, so they avoided producing any new antagonisms. There was a greater consensus as to the value of linguistics as background information for the teacher than as something to be taught directly. I believe that we succeeded in making the point that there is no such thing as a linguistic method of teaching English. There was clearly expressed, however, a desire for greater emphasis on the semantic component than there has been in the past, and I believe that there is some disposition around the country to share this view. The idea that any English teacher in his preparatory work should have been exposed to at least two systems of grammatical analysis, adopted subsequently in *Guidelines for the Preparation of Teachers of English*,[5] owes something to the tenor of the conversations at Dartmouth but this should not be interpreted too narrowly. There was some interest too in the application of linguistics to the analysis of literature, but again largely as a matter of information, another handle so to speak, rather than as a substitute for any current approach.

Early in my discussion I did indicate that there was some question in my mind about the actuality of a so-called new English. In a very strict sense of the term, I doubt that there is. Certainly we are not introducing new subject matter in the sense that the new mathematics introduced set theory at a point in the curriculum where it had not been dreamed of before. Nor are we selecting one or two divisions of the conventional subject matter of English to be explored in greater depth, as was the case with the new physics. Our concerns are still the development of a sensitivity to literature, some acquaintance with the literary heritage, and the ability to employ the language with competence and sincerity. If there is anything new in what has developed recently, it is in the concept of means rather than ends, in certain of our values and attitudes. I, for one, am quite satisfied with this state of affairs and firmly believe that it can justly be counted as advance toward a goal. I look at what has been going on as evolution and see this as a sounder basis for progress than revolution.

To sum up, it is difficult to arrive at any unified or overall conclusion about the impact of Dartmouth, especially upon language teaching. No single formulary statement is possible, no matter how ingeniously phrased. With respect to language, as with virtually every other aspect of English teaching, Dartmouth was germinal. It marked a significant step toward international cooperation. It recognized realistically that the agreement recorded there would not be final, and already with respect to language teaching, the situation has moved somewhat beyond it. Certainly the great and almost unique virtue of Dartmouth lay in its recognition that English was a problem for the future even more than for the present, and it is in this that I see the evolutionary ferment at work.

---

[1] These two films taken from BBC telecasts are available on a limited basis through the National Council of Teachers of English.

[2] *Teaching English in the United Kingdom*, A Comparative Study. James R. Squire and Roger K. Applebee. Champaign, Illinois: National Council of Teachers of English, 1969.

[3] Reprinted by permission of Alan S. C. Ross. "U and NON-U, An Essay in Sociological Linguistics," in *Noblesse Oblige*, edited by Nancy Mitford. New York: Harper & Row, 1956.

[4] A Dartmouth Conference pamphlet distributed to participants at the Richmond Institute. (Champaign, Illinois: National Council of Teachers of English, 1968.)

[5] *Guidelines for the Preparation of Teachers of English*. From *English Journal* (September 1967), *Elementary English* (October 1967), *College English* (October 1967). Champaign, Illinois: National Council of Teachers of English, 1967.

2

Education and the Fourth Reform

American education has undergone two major periods of reform and is at the present time in the midst of a third. The first of these was led by a group of Whig reformers and educators like Horace Mann and Henry Barnard, who saw schooling as a vehicle for maintaining political order and for raising moral standards. The second reform occurred at the turn of the present century, when industrialization, immigration, and a collapsing agricultural system caused a great population shift from rural areas to urban areas. As a consequence, new city dwellers were met by the devastating problems of inadequate housing, rapidly shifting political patterns, breakdowns in family structure, and grossly inade-

Edward Simpkins/Graduate Fellow, Harvard University/Presented at the Springfield Institute

quate police and social welfare facilities. Jacob Riis and Robert Hunter were among the journalists who challenged these problems by demanding food, clothing, and housing for the poor, and by insisting that the schools work together with social agencies. Their efforts led to the establishment of school lunch programs and to the cooperative identification of impoverished youngsters.

The third reform movement, a thrust for teachers' rights, gained impetus during the 1960s as militant teacher organizations across the country fought for and won the right to bargain collectively in all matters concerning wages, hours, and working conditions. Since that time teachers have turned in increasing numbers to collective bargaining as a means of gaining improved benefits, viable grievance procedures, and more recently, as a means of becoming involved in decisions that affect curriculum.

There are some educators who view collective bargaining as a technique to be used only for winning concessions on bread-and-butter issues. However, examination of a number of contracts negotiated by teachers reveals that they have won the right to: (1) review textbooks and curriculum guides, (2) set limitations on class size, (3) mandate the purchase of textbooks that portray a multiracial society, and (4) require boards of education to adopt plans designed to integrate school systems. Obviously, there are implications in collective bargaining in this third reform movement for English teachers, department chairmen, and language arts supervisors. Not too long ago an NCTE conference for department chairmen resulted in twenty-three recommendations for improving the status of English teaching. These ranged from making provisions for classroom teachers to become involved in curriculum decisions to giving chairmen a voice in recruitment and hiring. Significantly, not one of these recommendations lay beyond the scope of collective bargaining.

In maintaining that collective bargaining promises to be the most effective means of promoting change that we have had in the history of American education, I would remind you of how change in school procedures was initiated formerly. Using a pyramidal structure to represent the educational establishment, one notes that ideas for change appeared to flow invariably from the apex, which represents the administrative staff, to the base, which represents the teachers. Years of experience with this type of process generated the belief among teachers that they were powerless and insignificant insofar as the development of school policies and curriculum was concerned. Collective bargaining has changed this situation by extending teachers' rights and responsibilities. Teachers can now take part in determining school policies. But they are bound to support those policies they helped to formulate and to encourage their colleagues to support them also. For under collective bargaining teachers have a stronger commitment to education. As partners in the policy-making process, they are placing their professional judgment and competence on the line along with that of administrators. Seen from this point of view, collective bargaining can be considered a unifying factor that will bring about innovative changes in school systems more quickly and with a greater guarantee of general support than was previously possible.

The third reform could not have occurred at a more suitable time. Quite clearly the schools are confronted with a number of massive crises today. The central crisis is largely one of deteriorating confidence. Certainly it is in part attributable to the failing effort of educators to effect meaningful racial integration of the schools. It is also attributable to our general failure to provide every youngster, black or white, with the kinds of skills that enable him to compete, with a chance for success, in the world of work or in gaining admission to a college or university that will afford him the opportunity to pursue a professional career. And finally, it is attributable in part to what the National Advisory Committee on Civil Disorders has labeled as latent and active racist tendencies, reflected also in our schools through curriculums and textbooks which help to perpetuate discriminatory practices and to develop a climate that is characterized by the twin evils of poverty and ignorance.

It is my opinion that all of this says something of great importance to those of us who are teachers of English. For it is the skills that we teach which are the most reliable indices of the student's achievement and growth and the most prominent measures of his failure and of the general failure of education. When James S. Coleman *et al.* compiled their massive critique on the inequalities of outputs of the public schools, they used as their criteria data relating almost exclusively to the skills taught by teachers of English. Of course it was not the intent of that committee to place the blame for education's shortcomings on the shoulders of English teachers. Yet we would be remiss, it seems to me, not to see in these data and in data compiled on the achievement scores of school dropouts, the unemployed, and the one-fourth of American society who are at best marginal citizens, a very important caveat for anyone who is a career teacher in the language arts or English. To a very large extent it is our instruction which makes up the core of what stands for education in the United States.

Experienced teachers know that there are no panaceas, no easy answers for the multiple and complex problems which we must solve. But we must be willing to accept the growing disenchantment with the free public education system as an irresistible force and to accept whatever consequences must inevitably flow from that disenchantment. We must not look indifferently upon the tragedies of American education depicted in the Coleman study or in such works as Jonathan Kozol's *Death at an Early Age* or Nat Hentoff's *Our Children Are Dying*. Looking particularly at the English program and repeating that collective bargaining is not an end in itself but a means of attaining a measurably higher quality of language arts instruction, I propose three courses of action.

First, we must examine and attempt to scrutinize our own techniques and methodology within the classroom with a view toward bringing about pronounced improvements. Self-scrutiny is difficult for all of us. Perhaps no one is a good English teacher all of the time. We have good semesters and poor semesters, and we have some semesters when we shift from being good teachers to bad teachers as the bell rings and our favorite students leave the room to be replaced by students whom we regard as not really worth our efforts. Students may not like the books that we teach from, the papers we assign, or they may not like us as the teachers to whom they must report. Whatever the case may be, we must educate the hostile as well as the friendly and the student who wants no part of the English curriculum as well as the student who loves English, as Mario Fantini of the Ford Foundation points out.

Lenore Jacobson and Robert Rosenthal have observed that

when teachers take the attitude that the students are not worth their while (which is perhaps another way of assuming that they either do not want to learn or cannot learn), this attitude affects the student's achievement. Jacobson and Rosenthal conducted a study in which they found that experimenters working with rats which they had been led to believe were dull, had little success in teaching them. But the same experimenters working with rats which they believed to be bright had significant success. Not content to generalize from rats to humans, Rosenthal and Jacobson moved their experiment into a school located in the South San Francisco Unified School District. After administering an intelligence test, they made a random selection of students without any reference to the test results. But they identified twenty percent of the children in each classroom as pupils who were likely to undergo significant learning spurts during the year.

Once again, the self-fulfilling prophecy was confirmed, as those students who were designated as likely to experience significant learning spurts did just that, whether their standardized test scores indicated that they had high ability or low ability. In fact their gains were substantially higher than were the gains of students who were not so designated. Assuming that Rosenthal and Jacobson are right and that attitudes do have a major effect on learning in the classroom, I hold that one way to help alleviate the crisis in language arts teaching is to devise model programs in English teaching that will rely to a far greater extent than we currently rely today on the use of technology.

Not only is this my second point, it is what I refer to as the fourth reform movement in education. It will be a movement that will claim the right, indeed, the obligation, of schools to accomplish with technology the critical goals that remain unfulfilled through total reliance upon human efforts. We, as English teachers, should begin even now to encourage friends in collective bargaining units to explore ways of experimenting with computer devices and teaching machines as a means of improving language arts instruction, lest these decisions be preempted by outsiders.

Implied in this second course of action is a program that allows for structuring curriculum and differentiating staff functions within an English department so that students will stand a good chance of being placed with teachers who believe in them. We know that this is a real need. Many English classrooms are run to meet the needs of the teacher rather than the needs of students. When a teacher develops a two-week program on William Shakespeare, for example, it is neither because Shakespeare nor the students need it but because the teacher does. In an age when the output of literature in the English language is so tremendous, and when the bulk of that output is in the area of nonfiction rather than fiction, and when we are teaching a generation that is vitally interested in space exploration, boy-girl relationships, and the exciting world of here and now, unquestionably many of the cherished idols and the sacred cows of a generation ago cannot and should not be preserved. No school system can survive the endless boredom of a curriculum that lacks relevance.

We must somehow find a way also to stop the tendency of our English classes to develop an upside down picture of the normal relationship between people and the exercise of language skills. Dr. David M. Silverstone, of the University of Bridgeport, once conducted an informal study of how people spend an average day. He concluded that we spend 45 percent of our time listening, 30 percent speaking, 16 percent reading, and 9 percent writing. How do these proportions fit the English classroom environment? Certainly the student who talks 30 percent of the time is a troublemaker. If he reads 16 percent of the time, he is probably investing at least some of that reading time in literature that the teacher for one reason or another finds objectionable. And if he appears to be listening 45 percent of the time, we can only hope that he actually is.

The irrelevance of English classes is the fault of neither the student nor the teacher. They both inherited an educational system that was designed for an earlier age. It has a structural dependency on human effort, human patience, and human interest. Although these qualities are present in educators and in students, they are not always present at the same time between students and teachers who must interact within a classroom and inside a framework called *English*. There is presently some evidence to indicate that much of the memory work and information gathering that are part of the English program can be taught more effectively by computers or by teaching machines than by classroom teachers.

Recently the U.S. Office of Education concluded a two-year study in conjunction with the University of South Florida. Ninety-nine children from the Florida Public Schools and from institutions for the mentally retarded were used in the study. The children ranged in mental age from five to nine. One-third of the students were taught to read by teaching machines for fifteen minutes a day. Another third were given tutorial instruction for fifteen minutes a day. And the final third were taught using the established methodology and in a regular classroom setting. At the end of an eight-week period, the machine-taught children did nearly as well as the children who were given the individualized tutorial instruction. But what was surprising was that they far surpassed the thirty-three children who had been taught in a regular classroom setting. They also outstripped their own previous performance, learning from two to six times as many words as they had learned in four years under the old classroom instruction.

Another impressive result came out of this study. The machine-taught students remembered a large majority of the new words sixty days later; they showed significant improvement in reading and spelling, far surpassing the students who were taught in the regular classroom setting in performance of these skills. This study seems to indicate that tutorial experiences are most effective for teaching students subject matter but that a properly constructed program can provide the student with tutorial instruction through a machine.

I believe, however, that it is necessary to approach this matter of teaching machines with great caution. There is certainly no reason to fear that the machine will displace teachers. On the other hand, there is every reason to hope that machines will modify the various functions of the teaching staff in any given English department, and that is the third course of action I am advocating. There is every reason to hope that machines can free more teachers to perform tutorial service in the schools. I look to the day when at least one day out of the week, Tuesday for example, can be used exclusively for tutorial instruction. The differentiated English staff that I envision will include some teachers whose function it will be to supervise paraprofessionals and certain technicians who will become a part of the school staff as technology is added. These teachers will have time for tutoring. I also envision some teachers promoting the continuing growth of the English curriculum and assisting in the programming of new materials. I see other English teachers serving as faculty consultants in that they, perhaps, will keep abreast of this rapidly changing technology and of curriculum materials adaptable to their school. These should be available on an exchange basis and with consultants having a direct link with centrally located authorities who can facilitate the qualitative growth of a language arts program. And finally I envision some English teachers as language development consultants to the students.

The computer, of course, is no panacea. Dr. Anthony Oettinger of Harvard University points out that computerized instruction may be of little use to schools unless schools are able to reorganize in order to absorb it. And it is also good to remember that once the blackboard was hailed as the remarkable innovation that would revolutionize education, as were radio, television, and 16 millimeter projectors. So experience suggests caution in our aspirations. But the fact that teaching machines and computers are here to stay, when considered in conjunction with the fact that we are in urgent need of what they promise for the future, mandates that we English teachers take the lead in this developing area of technology. What I am suggesting is that teachers should be in the vanguard of the fourth reform, instead of waiting for engineers and publishing firms to guide the development of this technology which will later be adapted to the classroom in some fashion. Teachers, as the primary change-agents, should plan the language arts or English program on the assumption that teaching machines or various computer devices can be made to order—that they can be made to meet specific needs or to perform specific job functions in instructional areas. Like businessmen, industrialists, military officials, and medical authorities, teachers must learn to spell out in advance the kinds of technological innovations they are seeking.

One thing is clear to me. We must have the developing technology to help us multiply our effectiveness. Experiments and eventual adoption of such electronic aids will go on whether or not English teachers show an interest in their possible applications. Patrick Suppes of Stanford University estimates that well over one million, possibly ten million, students will be receiving computer-assisted instruction within the next ten years. Even today some students are involved in a number of experimental programs. The results of these have not been disclosed; however, it is generally agreed that under properly structured conditions the computer-assisted instruction shows a marked superiority over the current procedures and methodology in the teaching of facts and reading skills, as well as in evaluating progress in these areas.

In concluding, I wish to cite several results that we, as English teachers, might want technology to accomplish for us. I would like to see technology help bring about classrooms that are alive with action, with boys and girls talking to their language arts consultant in a friendly atmosphere, individually, or in small groups where true exchanges may occur. I use the term *language arts consultant* purposely. I believe that among the changes that should occur in teaching is a change in titles, which will help define the new roles and job functions which teachers will perform. In my model, the student would work with machines that would be constantly receiving up-to-date programs. Literature would be much more current than it is now, and the teachers—language arts consultants—would have as a major part of their own responsibility keeping abreast of what is new in literature so that they could develop language materials based on current literature for use in the classroom.

The language arts consultants to whom the students would go would be rewarded with knowledgeable students who would come into the discussion-study not only unafraid to talk and to write, but often with something written which teachers could read and react to. This system would certainly help to put an end to the embarrassment of students that occurs when they are forced to take part in discussions when they actually have nothing to contribute. In the model I propose, students would talk, because they would only visit the consultant for an oral examination on subject matter when the self-test results from the computer program indicated that they had a sufficient knowledge of the subject to meet and discuss its content with their assigned consultant. When students do not talk in class today, it is because they have nothing to say. They do not write for the same reason. They tell us this but we pretend not to believe them. On occasion, we try to get them to make some innocuous remarks and pretend that we will accept any kind of an utterance as a contribution. Despite the fact that we may be sincere, or perhaps just desperate, when we do this, the student realizes that innocuous remarks are not real contributions unless they are being made to a psychiatrist. And if we insist on the student making an innocuous remark, it is because we need it not the student. He wants to be relevant to the situation. If he is talking to a language arts consultant, then he wants to be able to talk about poetry or grammar. That is why I favor a model that permits the student to acquire some degree of mastery and to undergo an immediate confidential test before he has to talk about the teacher's specialty with him.

Another important feature of my model is that the literature would be individualized during the last year of the student's English program. I want a machine that can allow for the programming of new materials for the school. I want to be able to program perhaps one hundred new books a semester so that students and parents can take part in language curriculum development. I want a machine that will allow a group of students to structure their own course in American literature or space travel or in a number of subject areas during their final year. And when that program is no longer relevant, I want to be able to file it away easily and make another one.

In this model teachers should have flexible schedules so that they can provide the necessary tutorial service on the one-to-one basis that will certainly be necessary. All students will not like computerized instruction. Some will daydream while pretending to be working at a computer. Certainly it is naive to assume that students will be good little boys and girls just because technology is added to the classroom. So in my model we would assign every student to Tuesday tutoring sessions at least twice a month, and every teacher, or language arts consultant, would be required to tutor six students in either reading or in writing.

The physical appearance of tutoring rooms and classrooms would be changed drastically from the appearance which they have today. I believe that the greatest shortcoming of English classrooms is that they rarely offer more than a hint of what is being taught in them. In 1935, S. G. Dulsky wrote in the *Journal of Experimental Psychology* that he had conducted a test which indicated that physical surroundings affect one's ability to acquire verbal skills. He went so far as to say that since learning takes place in the classroom, there will be some association of learned materials in that particular environment, and if we wish to enhance recall of learned material later in the real world, classrooms should look less like schoolrooms and more like office buildings, factories, homes, or whatever environment to which the materials learned are to apply. Even though I have serious questions about the full applicability of Mr. Dulsky's data, I believe that language laboratories ought to vary in accord with the language experiences that go on in them. Cubicles that resemble a series of phone booths are fine when students are getting individualized machine instruction. But in my model there would be more than one kind of a language laboratory. The consultation room for language arts students would look more like a study or a living room than a classroom. There would be newspapers on end tables and perhaps carpeting on the floor. The language arts consultant would meet there with small groups of students, and they would discuss matters relating to the curriculum on an individual basis or as a group. If some students carried on a conversation with each other while the language arts consultant was talking with another person, there would be no need to demand silence.

Another language laboratory would look like a lecture room. Students who were concentrating their literature experiences in subject areas like chess or space travel or Afro-American history would, upon application or by invitation, be scheduled to speak in an established student-lecture series. After all, some of our students are junior experts in intellectual areas just as they are junior experts in certain sports. Some language laboratories would look like conference rooms and some would look like radio and television stations. Just as science rooms seem to say *science* to visitors to the school, just as home economics rooms seem to say *home economics,* just as music rooms seem to say *music*—the language arts rooms would seem to say *conversation, broadcasting, literature,* or *seminar.*

In my model, the language arts consultant would, from time to time, occupy a variety of lateral positions which would provide for a diversity of functions that are not built into the present system.

At times he might work with youngsters as a consultant, and at other times as a researcher for his colleagues reading literature for the development of new programs. At still other times he might be a full-time tutor or a supervisor of technicians and/or paraprofessionals who would work under him in computer-assisted instruction.

Because of the wide range of responsibilities he would have, he would also be given some time to do the reading and the writing which would be expected of him. He might, for example, have to spend a day at a university or at a library for study and self-improvement, and in my model of the fourth reform this would be encouraged. English teachers or consultants in the language arts would be expected to read and write and practice all of the skills that they teach. As I envision the fourth reform, no one would be upset if English teachers took a day off occasionally for professional service or improvement—that is, as long as they did not take Tuesdays off, because Tuesdays are for tutoring.

3

Base for Creative Affirmation

Perhaps at no other time has the social temper of a period spirited the need for school curriculum reform as it has in the last several years. Unlike the demand for accelerated curriculum reformation which followed the successful launching of the first Russian satellite in the fall of 1957 or which followed World War II when the test scores of young recruits for the armed services "revealed shocking inadequacies in the science and mathematical programs of high-school graduates," [1] modern societal demands have added new dimensions both in breadth and in depth.

Whereas previous demands for curriculum reforms were concerned almost exclusively with the "talented tenth" of the school

Delores Minor/Detroit Public Schools/Presented at the Santa Barbara Institute

population, today our social and moral concerns reflect our commitment to the socio-economically and culturally deprived. This large segment of our population individually and collectively is asserting massive drives for power in the structure of education, especially in large urban settings. What happens as a result of this group's urgings will have implications for educators in all school settings.

Edgar Z. Friedenberg aptly highlights the rationale for schools reaching the culturally deprived potential dropout.

> The school . . . would have to take lower class life seriously as a condition and a pattern of experience, not just as a contemptible and humiliating set of circumstances that every decent boy or girl is anxious to escape from. It would have to accept their language, their dress, and their values as a point of departure for disciplined exploration, to be understood not as a trick for luring them into the middle class but as a way of helping them to explore the meaning of their own lives. This is the way to encourage and nurture potentialities from *whatever* social class.[2]

In essence, the area between the concreteness of life in the ghetto and the abstractness and meaninglessness of the curriculum has to be bridged if the school is to become a functional part of the student's life. As Jean Grambs relates,

> The school demands of children that they deny what their own sense experiences tell them and accept instead the school's version of reality. They may be making such an effort to meet this demand that in the process they have little energy left with which to learn the content that is offered them.[3]

By its very nature, its complexities, its educational, social, and economic needs, the inner city is ripe as a base for creative, imaginative teaching and learning. The challenge is there; the raw materials are there. One superintendent describes this raw material as

> a victim of his environment. The ghetto child begins his school career psychologically, socially, and physically disadvantaged. He is oriented to the present rather than the future, to immediate needs rather than delayed gratification, to the concrete rather than the

abstract. He is often handicapped by limited cognitive skills, low self-esteem, and a stunted drive toward achievement.[4]

Perhaps the most serious deficiency of the deprived person is his feeling of inadequacy; unfortunately, the effects of his adverse experiences do not stop even here. The majority of these students are black and have already undergone the process of survival in their intimate experiences with discrimination, relative deprivation, and rejection. However, when deprived students enter the schoolroom, their middle-class teachers demand middle-class standards in dress, rhetoric, code of behavior, and conformity. In his introduction to *The Culturally Deprived Child*, Goodwin Watson assesses the peculiarities of this school composition:

> The American public school is a curious hybrid: it is managed by a school board drawn largely from upper-class circles; it is taught by teachers who come from middle-class backgrounds; and it is attended mainly by children from working-class homes. These three groups do not talk the same language. They differ in their manner, power, and hierarchies of values.[5]

The result very often is a large number of alienated students whose academic performance decreases as feelings of alienation and rejection increase. Students begin to lose faith in the school as an agent concerned about them and their educational growth; their parents begin to decry the seeming apathy of the school and demand that it assume a responsible share in what their children learn and how they learn it.

What a base for the creative affirmation of teachers committed to the functional and developmental growth of the young people! Such a base can be realized if the following three conditions are implemented.

1. *If attitudes of teachers and administrators undergo a process of change, a kind of lobotomy.*

Each person must undergo some mental anguish in his own mind and heart as he listens to that small voice that speaks to him to refrain from responding to differences, especially when the object of the differences is singled out by color.

A person may insist on his virtue as a respecter of people

simply because both share the bonds of humanity. However, if he asks the question, How do you teach black students?, it is one indication that he has not yet discovered the *I* in his own being and therefore does not recognize the *I* in another. He has not yet learned to cope with the differences openly and sensitively; nor has he learned that students are students for "a' that and a' that."

No one reaches his humanity the easy way; however, the directions are clear if he first of all has a knowledge and understanding of the problems and the nature of young people. According to a recent survey of more than 50,000 teenagers in a study by Dr. Merton P. Strommen, executive director of Church Youth Research in Minneapolis, teenagers consider their number one problem their view of themselves. According to the report, "Many teenagers believe they don't have what it takes to establish themselves as respected, contributing members of our fast-moving society." [6] The second problem teenagers reported is their fear of rejection by their peer groups. An important aspect of the study is that teachers, responding to the same survey the way *they* thought young people would answer, consistently misinterpreted teenagers' feelings and attitudes.

Margaret Mead explains that young people today are

> creatures of another kind. Youth are the natives in this new technological land and all those over 25 are foreigners. It is as if one group is speaking Japanese and one is speaking English and they are under the illusion they are talking the same language. Young people are lonely and frightened because they know they must find a better way of running the world, but they have no wise men to turn to.[7]

Young black students, part of this group, bring to it their unique problems of being black in a white-structured society. They bring Ellison's antihero's "hurt to the point of abysmal pain, hurt to the point of invisibility."[8]

It remains, then, for the teacher and the administrator to rid themselves of the myth barrier and the color block, both of which hinder acceptance of a large segment of the population.

2. *If English programs and procedures are revised to be of this point in time.*

To reach the vast number of disinherited students, English programs must be varied and inductively taught, and they must at least begin with a content that is specific, pertinent, and visual.[9] To be effective, teachers must approach their subject in a manner which relates to this learning style of students.

In discussing one of the causes of irrelevance in education and suggested levels for achieving relevance, Mario D. Fantini and Gerald Weinstein conclude that

> irrelevance is caused if teaching procedures and learning styles are not matched. The current literature on disadvantaged children indicates that they learn best in more concrete, inductive, kinesthetic, and less verbal situations. In view of this, their teachers should search for methodology coordinated with this learning style. Thus, if all techniques, practices and methods used by teachers are geared specifically to the pupil's own style of learning, then, regardless of content there is a degree of relevance in whatever is being taught because of HOW it is being taught.[10]

Lecturing and insisting that students take notes will not suffice; having students read and answer end-of-lesson questions will not suffice. The approach must be one in which the teacher is more concerned with the *why* rather than with the *what*, in which the teacher provides opportunities for the students to become actively involved in *doing* something and to feel a sense of accomplishment in the doing.

3. *If schools offer multiple programs within the curriculum rather than the single concept structure of remediation.*

Humanities programs, individualized instruction, problem-solving classes, learning center, electives—each offers unique outlets for the learner to strengthen his image and to add to his humanistic education.

The consistency with which programs for the disadvantaged focus on cognitive learning at the exclusion of the affective response is cause for some concern. Since many programs for the disadvantaged are federally supported, it is noteworthy that successful 1969 ESEA Title I programs were those which emphasized cognitive gains, as evaluated by the American Institute on

Research in consultation with the National Advisory Council on the Education of Disadvantaged Children. A note of optimism, however, appears in one of the recommendations of the Council: "We urge professionals to move beyond cognitive achievement tests and into other realms . . . self-concept, creativity, motivation, behavior . . . where compensatory education programs may have equally important long-range results." [11]

Since inner-city education, along with its components and its implications, is one of the major imperatives in the overall improvement of education, we not only can establish it as a base for creative teaching, we must. We no longer have a choice. The hearts and minds of too many people, white and black, are at stake, as indeed is the survival of a nation.

And in case any educator would question the implications of this imperative for himself and his school, let him read the White Plains Study, which warns, "A different type of education is going to have to be forged for all youth." [12] Let him read the highlights of the 1969 annual meeting of the National Association of Secondary School Principals. Let him analyze his own school to determine if he has any student with educational disabilities and if he has any minority student whose problems are compounded mainly because of race.

The saving grace may be that the inner city admits to—indeed clamors about—its poor education and is bent on recouping the losses, whether others like it or not.

No one can say with any degree of impunity that he has no problem simply because he teaches in the suburbs, or in a nice, little, wealthy school in a semirural district, or in an all-white school in a large city, or in a school that has few blacks or students from other minority groups. All schools are vulnerable, even if they do no more than provide an environment for student attacks on the establishment. And students are aware of the social revolution in America, though they may understand it only at an abstract level. Whether or not the teacher in such schools feels a need to deal with the social revolution in his classes, he must know that his students encounter it constantly if they watch television.

We can afford neither to delude ourselves nor to take refuge in escape; either defense gives only temporary relief and does grave psychological damage in the process. There is no place to hide. It is imperative that students and teachers in school situations with no "social problems" become aware of and study the literature and cultural heritage of blacks and other minority groups. Such study offers one of our few hopes of expanding students' perception of humanity through giving them a chance to see the characteristics they share with all people and an opportunity to participate imaginatively in the lives of others whom they would only rarely encounter in their own culture.

In focusing on curriculum reforms for the education of the educationally handicapped, we must have foresight and perseverance; we must be prepared to work toward changes consistent with our concern for human understanding and a humanistic curriculum. In addition, we must work diligently to implement these concerns:

1. Administration and curriculum leaders must come together in the common interest of the learner. Each group should have clearly defined lines of authority; the two groups should have a good working rapport.
2. We must become aware of research in linguistics, pertinent to speech and reading especially, and determine how to implement the findings.
3. Educators must work to build a more accurate image of themselves in the community and work to maintain it throughout the year, every year. The effect of good P.R. should never be minimized.
4. We must study ways, means, and proposals for change in present systems of evaluation and grading. Clearly, with new emphases being added to courses—old and new—criteria and grading symbols as we know them cannot be used effectively. They are misleading, stifling, and obscure.
5. We must address ourselves to the development of human skills even to the point of agitating for completely restructured schools. In our mechanistic society, nowhere is the emphasis on human skills more essential than in the schools.

Ralph Ellison in his *Invisible Man* speaks about humanity. His discussion can easily be applied to the present state of education in the United States.

Life is to be lived, not controlled; and humanity is won by continuing to play in the face of certain defeat. Our fate is to become one, and yet many—This is not prophecy, but description. Thus one of the greatest jokes in the world is the spectacle of the whites busy escaping blackness and becoming blacker every day, and the black striving toward whiteness, becoming quite dull and gray. None of us seems to know who he is or where he's going.[13]

When we do find out, perhaps we as well as our students will be prepared not for a capital B for Black or a capital W for White, but for "a capital H for Human." [14]

---

[1] John I. Goodlad. "The Reform Movement," *School Curriculum Reform in the United States*. (New York: The Fund for the Advancement of Education, 1964), p. 9.

[2] Edgar Z. Friedenberg. "An Ideology of School Withdrawal," *The School Dropout*, edited by Daniel Schreiber (Washington, D.C.: NEA, 1964), p. 38.

[3] Jean D. Grambs. *Schools, Scholars and Society* (New York: Prentice-Hall, 1965), p. 80.

[4] Reprinted with permission from "The Inner City—A Superintendent's View," by Carl J. Dolce, January 11, 1969 *Saturday Review*. Copyright © 1969 Saturday Review, Inc., New York.

[5] Reprinted with permission from Goodwin Watson's introduction to Frank Riessman's *The Culturally Deprived Child*, published by Harper & Row, Publishers, Inc., New York. Copyright © 1962.

[6] "What's Bugging Today's Teenagers?" *Scholastic Teacher* (February 7, 1969), p. 7.

[7] From a speech by Margaret Mead at Columbia University Teachers College Annual Dinner, summarized in *Education U.S.A.* (March 3, 1969, p. 147), Copyright © 1969 National School Public Relations Association.

[8] Reprinted with permission from *Invisible Man* by Ralph Ellison, published by Random House, Inc., New York. Copyright © 1952.

[9] Reprinted with permission from *The Culturally Deprived Child* by Frank Riessman, published by Harper & Row, Publishers, Inc., New York. Copyright © 1962.

[10] Reprinted by permission of the Anti-Defamation League of B'nai B'rith.

[11] The National Advisory Council on the Education of Disadvantaged Children, *Title I—ESEA: A Review and a Forward Look—1969*, Fourth Annual Report, (Washington, D.C.: Office of Education, 1969), p. 24.

[12] Dan W. Dodson, *High School Racial Confrontation: A Study of the White Plains, New York, Student Boycott* (Washington, D.C.: U.S. Commission on Civil Rights, 1969), p. 57.

[13] Reprinted with permission from *Invisible Man* by Ralph Ellison, published by Random House, Inc., New York. Copyright © 1952.

[14] John Ciardi, "Manner of Speaking," *Saturday Review* (January 11, 1969), p. 95.

4

Creativity

Creativity is the new cant—parents are advised not to hit it with
a stick, schoolteachers are primed to watch for it, foundations encourage it, colleges and subsidized health farms nourish it in a regu-
lated atmosphere; the government is advised to honor it . . . the
creativity con-game is a great subject for comedy.[1]

T hat refreshing breath of cool sense is from Pauline Kael's review
of Federico Fellini's 8½, a film about a creative person, in this
case a film director, and about the way in which he is seen to
be creative. Pauline Kael's response, to see the film as related to, as
a manifestation of, cant, seems to me to be perfectly fair; because at
no time do we see the star of the film, the creative person, involved

Geoffrey Summerfield/University of York/Presented at the St.
Louis Institute

in any of those activities that are a part of creative activity: planning, shaping, experimenting, playing with the medium, discussing, working things out, modifying, rejecting, learning from others, practising his art, and so on. He simply sits around listlessly like a romantic poet, or tumbles into bed with his mistress, or takes a turkish bath—all this while waiting for that magical commodity, inspiration. If for no reason other than this, the film is a silly and banal fantasy. And yet as evidence of the layman's notions of creative activity, the film is extremely significant: hailed and acclaimed as a profound insight into the nature of the creative individual, it merely projected the same old stereotype of the creative person that has been with us ever since the late 18th century when the bards began to grow their hair long and journey up to the mist-wreathed mountaintops to commune with the muse. This stereotype, or myth, depends on a romantic and fatalistic psychology—"poeta nascitur, non fit": poets, creative types, are born, not made. That's the way the genetic cooky crumbles, and there's nothing anybody can do about it. Such a psychology is not merely fatalistic; it is also conservative, not to say reactionary. For it rests on the assumption that somehow or other, in more or less arcane, mysterious, and esoteric fashion, the universe conspires to give birth to X number of creative persons: and their existence, as such, has nothing whatever to do with the system, social, political, or economic, though the survival of the creative individual may well be contingent upon that system.

Now the argument that rests upon the pious acceptance of the cosmic dictate—That's the way they're made and there's nothing we can do about it—occurs in other contexts, apparently dissimilar but essentially, in terms of the dominant, current conception of man, essentially the same. When Indian adolescents are sadistically mistreated in a boarding school in the Midwest and the scandalous depravity of the school faculty is revealed, the defense of the faculty, the rationalization of their brutal treatment of their charges, is couched in the following terms: "But what can you expect: they're *only* Indians." Now this "they're *only* so-and-sos" formulation occurs whenever those in power reach for a justification of their destruction, either literal or metaphorical, either physical or spiritual, of other human beings. In Nazi Germany, as the bodies were buried in lime pits or burned to ashes, "They're only Jews"; in the

American South, "They're only niggers"; in Steinbeck's account of the mistreatment of migrant workers in California in the 30s, "They're only Okies"; in the 60s, "They're only Mexicans"; in many an English high school, "They're only slum kids."

Now, beneath the ostensibly disconnected there lurk profound and subtle connections: and the society that is primarily concerned with the efficiently punitive treatment of delinquent adolescents, with refinements of punishment, with suppression of dissent, is the same society that consistently underrates its also-rans, its burgeoning dropouts, its occupants of the lower tracks. And the school system that has a low level of expectation of its socially and economically poor students, that writes them off as dropouts, is passing judgment not on the students but on itself: so when we say of a student as he is about to leave school: "He never did anything worthwhile," we are describing our own failure, the failure of the system, the self-fulfilling prophecies that we have visited on that student more or less from the beginning of his school life.

The evidence lies all around us, but many of us prefer not to observe it because to do so would probably involve us in some agonizing reappraisal of what we are being paid for. In England we organize such self-deception, such counterrevolution, with clumsy ingenuity. (Clumsy, because it's psychologically crude and humanly insensitive; ingenuity, because we can always find reasons for justifying what we do.) We put the poorer kids in the D stream, the bottom track, from the age of eight: such kids, by our definition, are D-stream pupils; and we know what to expect of D-stream pupils—underachievement, lassitude, restlessness, insubordination, disobedience, dirty fingernails, and failure to perform the tricks that our acceptable pupils learn very quickly to perform.

Yet, that it can be otherwise we must also, by this time, recognize: the evidence, again, is all around us. In England, to take only one example, it is to be found in Tom Haggit's book, *Working with Language:* this is an honest account of work in an elementary school with children of slum origins, children of barely literate parents: the evidence of the batteries of objective standardized tests suggested that the average I.Q. of the school population worked out at something below 100; but the staff agreed to work with very high expectations of these children. "Let's assume," they suggested, "that these kids can do the kinds of things that teachers on the posh side of town might expect of *their* pupils." [2] The results were, in a word, startling: when I visited the school, on every occasion I saw these poor children writing novels, stories, poems, journals, observations, accounts of experiments, and in other modes: and the products of these children were uniformly extraordinary: and "extraordinary," please note, is not an absolute but a relative: their novels, for example, were extraordinary simply because the ordinary, what we commonly expect, is less than the kids are actually capable of. So that when we use such a term as *extraordinary* or *incredible*, we are saying a great deal about our own habitual expectations.

Come nearer home and what do we find? Let's stop not at the middling level but at the bottom, not just at the level of dropouts even, but at the level of the pariahs, the criminals, the social rejects. Consider, for example, Thomas Merton's description of Harlem:

> Here in this huge, dark, steaming slum, hundreds of thousands of Negroes are herded together like cattle, most of them with nothing to eat and nothing to do . . . in this huge cauldron, inestimable natural gifts, wisdom, love, music, science, poetry are stamped down and left to boil with the dregs of an elementally corrupted nature, and thousands upon thousands of souls are destroyed by vice and misery and degradation, obliterated, wiped out, washed from the register of the living, dehumanized.[3]

Yet, after all that, what do many of the inmates of the American prisons want most to do? To read and to write. Thoreau, in Concord jail in 1846. Eldridge Cleaver in Folsom Prison in the 1960s. And some, because they have something that they want desperately and urgently to say, write like angels. Eldridge Cleaver, for example, seems to me—in the range of his wit, his gaiety, his resonant sense of tragedy, his zest, his rhythm, his psychological penetration—to come closer to D. H. Lawrence than anyone since 1931. And in his essay "On Becoming" in *Soul on Ice* he tells us why he started to write: "To save myself."

But in America as in England, only more so I venture to surmise, you have this paradox: that whilst the glory of man is in instinctiveness, in what Gerard Manley Hopkins called *inscape* (and it's interesting, for it tells us something about our own recent history, that he had to coin a word for the occasion); whilst, as Shapiro puts it, "all true poems are equal in truth and separate in truth"; whilst the glory of the American continent is in the diversity of cultures within its borders; whilst we apprehend the reality of another person in apprehending his otherness; whilst all this seems to me true, and importantly so; yet, the system of which we are members, the socio-political philosophy of which we are writing or for which we act as unwitting agents, these appear to be dedicated to the neutralization, the processing, of the individual. And at the root of such a dreary dedication seems to me to lie an unexamined intolerance, an unconscious xenophobia. We simply can't bear it, that others should be unlike ourselves, should do, not our, but their thing. So in New Orleans, for example, black children in the first grade are being drilled in "I saw" as a replacement for "I seen": not in an intelligent and explicit form of bilingualism, but in the spirit of a shibboleth.

Any attempt, therefore, to consider creativity *in vacuo,* whether psychologically or socially, is doomed to failure: it must fail on account of its naïveté, on account of its abstraction, on account of its failure to live with the proper burden of social awareness. (If the system is geared to the promotion of social and linguistic conformity, and geared primarily or exclusively to such ends, then that system will not tolerate, cannot include, teaching which is conducive to vividly human ends.)

I'd like to turn now to practical and pedagogical matters and to begin by quoting from Edward Rosenheim's lecture, which appears in *The Shape of English.*

> I wonder whether education can seek any higher goal than the cultivation of a capacity to use our uniquely human gifts for the achievement of uniquely human satisfactions. And if it be argued that no one needs to be "trained" to enjoy the things of this life, I would reply that the deepest, most distinctively human pleasures are precisely those which arise from the active, energetic, *cultivated* employment of our human endowments—which is precisely what is implied by the word "training." [4]

For the sake of my present argument, I wish to accept Edward Rosenheim's formulation—"the active, energetic, cultivated employment of our human endowments"—as a conveniently brief way of describing or presenting what we, as teachers of English, ought to be concerned with: our job, professionally, is to set up situations in our classrooms which will foster or promote "the active, energetic, cultivated employment of our human endowments."

And since we are teachers of English, we can justifiably delimit the area of those human endowments that we are here to promote: the endowment of speech, the endowment of hearing, and those more emphatically cultural endowments of writing and reading and of symbol-making, representing the world and our sense of it in symbolic form. In real life, we are doing such things constantly, in making conversation, in engaging in discussion and argument, in writing letters, in recounting pleasurable or painful experiences to our friends, in anticipating, rehearsing, and preparing ourselves for the next day, in daydreaming and indulging in fantasy: such are the natural out-of-school activities of our lives; on top of which we find such things as watching television, building a fence, mending a broken toy, reading a book, dancing, and so on. Now, for me, the key word in Rosenheim's phrase is the term *employment*. Consider, for example, the activity of two men collaborating in the building of a boat: if they already possess the basic skills and insights, if they are concerned to do a good job, and if they have adequate and appropriate materials, they will succeed in building a respectable boat. When they are actually planing, sawing, and so on, they are *employing* their skills—their manual, craft skills. When they are talking about it, they are not doing it; but their training will have been all the more sufficient to meet their needs if it has involved both doing and talking about doing, talking of a preparatory or planning kind, talking of a simultaneous parallel kind that accompanies, regulates, and controls the doing as it is a-doing, talking of a forensic, evaluative, critical kind that serves both to modify, if necessary, the job already done, and also to regulate or guide future exercises of skill.

Now, we don't know nearly enough about these uses of language, but what we do know is that they take place, that they are necessary, and that they are not performed simply as a gratuitous intellectual or linguistic game. The performance, the employment,

is both manual (sensory-motor) and linguistic: and the employment fares forward to a desired end.

If we have gone wrong in the past—and I think that we have
gone wrong—it is in having a false social philosophy and in having
a false notion of the ways in which to foster linguistic attainments.
On top of all this we've had a wrong or inappropriate notion of
such linguistic attainments—we have set for our pupils the wrong
goals, and we have often set them up at the wrong time. The false
social philosophy lay in our categorically separating off, in a rigid
manner, the creative artists from the rest of us: all human beings
are creative when allowed or encouraged to be so.

To foster linguistic attainments, we have neglected the bedrock
fact that linguistic attainment is fostered by employment rather
than by analysis. And our wrong-headed notion of linguistic attainment has rested on the assumption—which we can now see to have
almost irresistible historical causes—the assumption that our goal
is the standard dialect, the standard orthography, and the standard
pointing-system in writing.

And we have set up such goals at the wrong time in that we
have bothered and nagged and prodded and red-pencilled our
pupils into an undue preoccupation with the niceties of form, of
decorum, and of propriety when such considerations were both
conceptually beyond their cognitive grasp and affectively trivial or
meaningless.

And we are going to make similar mistakes with creativity: we
are going to treat it as something very special, as something that is
reducible to having the kids perform special, odd, bizarre tricks,
like writing haiku on Tuesday afternoons: instead of regarding it
rather as a continuous and continuing stance, a stance vis-à-vis
experience, as a way of responding to the fact of being alive and as
a way of responding to the fact that we are social animals: the
representations that we make of the world and of ourselves to
others—whether it's a joke, an anecdote, a story, a novel, an improvisation in drama, or a poem—these representations are also
presentations, which we present to others for their acceptance.
When our presentations are accepted, so are we accepted. And it
was a native son of St. Louis who wrote wise words about the

importance of acceptance and of acceptedness, as you will doubt-
less recall if you know T.S. Eliot's *Four Quartets*.

Let me finish with a short story.

Karen: The Bird
One day, I saw a bright collored bird. He was a black shiny bird
with a red spot on his wing. He was sitting in a field of corn. He
seemed to be talking to other birds all over the field, and waiting
for their reply. I tried to catch him but he flew away. I looked over
the field many times, before I found him. When I saw him the last
time he was happy and gay, now he had a broken wing. I was very
unhappy, so I took the bird in my hand and then took my sweater
and made a soft bed for him. I took him home with me. I begged my
mother to let me take care of him. She said yes. Three weeks had
past I fed him and kept him in a box, he seemed to be getting well.
One day, I went to his box he was gone. I looked all over the house
and found him in the upstairs bathroom. I then took him in my hand
and took him back to the place where I found him and then I went
home. When I got there he was sitting his box. So I kept him tell
he died seven years later. It is said that you can't tame the wild. But
it is possible.

I end with this, not because it is exceptional but precisely because it is not exceptional; a story by a sixth-grade student, written
for a first-grade class.

---

[1] Reprinted with permission from *I Lost It at the Movies* by Pauline Kael,
published by Little, Brown and Company, Boston. Copyright © 1965.

[2] Reprinted with permission from *Working with Language* by Tom Haggit,
published by Basil Blackwell, Oxford, England. Copyright © 1967.

[3] Reprinted with permission from *Secular Journal* by Thomas Merton,
published by Farrar, Straus & Giroux, New York. Copyright © 1959.

[4] *The Shape of English*, NCTE 1967 Distinguished Lectures, published by
the National Council of Teachers of English, Champaign, Illinois.

5

Who Let the Students In?

We did. And now that they storm about on what we are accustomed to considering our turf, some of us are confounded, confused, even hurt. They do not seem to be grateful to be there.

For much longer than has not been the case, we teachers and administrators have always known whom the schools belonged to. They were ours! We made policy in the best interests of the student; we implemented it. And in all of this we took for granted the then-silent and acquiescent student body.

If they were unhappy about things, the things tended to be matters known to be nonessential: the kinds of records played in

Ernece B. Kelly/Chicago City College, Loop Campus/Presented at the Richmond Institute

the lunchroom, the ban on smoking, or the rationing of Ping-pong balls. Few of us ever seriously entertained the idea of students organizing like other depressed and deprived groups to articulate their grievances.

Indeed, few of us are even now willing to demolish our favored stereotypes of the high schooler. We insist on seeing only the transistor-carrying fellows or the ones driving cars plastered with nicknames and bright flowers or the girls lugging notebooks scrawled with cryptic declarations of who loves whom. These accoutrements of youth probably will not change significantly. For young people seem to be generally less afraid to manifest their affection for rhythms and melody, their fascination with high speeds and fast stops, and their love of being in love.

But there is more to the youth culture than those externals. There always was, but previously it was easier to ignore. Never before was 42 percent of the population below the age of twenty-one; never before were there so many environmental factors kindling young people's outspokenness; never before have so many nonviolent tactics been part of their everyday language. And language does, indeed, assist in shaping the actualities and possibilities of their worlds.

Even now, tenaciously gripping the favored stereotypes, some of us refuse to believe that protest is happening because of the students or that it is happening to us. We blame those omniscient outside agitators and variously call up the spectre of Communists, local gangs, or the Black Panthers. Conveniently, we exempt ourselves—with a rapidity that suggests its source is instinctual—from those teachers whose work practices are right now being called irrelevant or superficial or racist.

In a speech recently given at the Illinois Association of Student Councils, the principal of a New York high school commented that our American system of education "evolved to serve an older, less individualistic or issues-conscious type of student, and these schools need change to meet this generation's need for active rather than passive learning." I'm convinced that he's right. But I don't see how teachers and administrators are going to reach students unless they have a clear idea of where they're at.

Commonly, one of the chief problems with the typical high

school is that it affords more opportunity for the teachers' observation of than for their identification with the less obvious characteristics of students. And I use *identification* in the same way Henry Saltzman does in his essay, "The Community School in the Urban Setting." It means more than understanding, for understanding is cerebral, whereas identification is partly visceral. Identification means caring about, respecting, and valuing those qualities which are characteristic of youth.

As long as we lord over our subjects in the classroom, as long as we cow them in the halls, we are neither inviting nor allowing full expression on the student's part. Usually the teachers hide in their own lunchroom when the Golden Hour of Liberation—the lunch hour—rolls around. This general behavior pattern suggests that teachers do not want to know their students. It even raises the question of whether teachers want to provide the time or the opportunity for students to truly get to know themselves.

Considering the remarkable changes students across this nation are initiating in their schools, we should be grateful to them. The least we can do is to attempt to know who and what they are. We can't do that with our comfortable stereotypes. And we can use their music as a battering-ram to break through those old images and to break into a wider arena of freedom for all of us.

Our students come to class having grooved on songs which deal with social problems, existential ways of looking at life, and fragments of thought which seem more appropriate to a philosophy book. And if we're still cranking up the phonograph, tuning in the Andrews Sisters or Perry Como, we're just not where the students are. And on one level that is all right.

There are at least two sound reasons why teachers shouldn't emerge en masse wearing see-through shirts and popping their fingers to the Rolling Stones. First, I suspect most students wouldn't trust them. And second, copying is probably the cheapest and, paradoxically, the most expensive way ultimately, to attempt identification with students. It is expensive because we cannot give them much of significance if we are too much like them.

I think social critic Paul Goodman describes an excellent middle ground between assuming the guise of teenagers and that polar stance of secure remoteness from them. He writes, "I had influence among them because, although I paid attention to them, I had a life of my own. I was not interested in being a leader of anyone, toward anything."

It's critical in today's atmosphere of change to realize the finite number of roles which delimit the teacher's identification with his students. Similarly, it's critical to appreciate what the odds are against any teacher breaking through the walls of inertia and stultification which hold up the roof of our typical school.

James Herndon describes those walls vividly in his book *The Way It Spozed to Be:*

> Sitting in a classroom or a home pretending to "study" a badly written text full of false information, adding up twenty sums when they're all the same and one would do, being bottled up for seven hours a day in a place where you decide nothing, having your success or failure depend, a hundred times a day, on the plan, invention and whim of someone else, being put in a position where most of your real desires are not only ignored but actively penalized, undertaking nothing for its own sake but only for that illusory carrot of the future. . . .

The problems in that description are compounded when we face a classroom peopled with Puerto Ricans, American Indians, Mexican-Americans, and blacks. An eighteen-year-old Puerto Rican describes the world he and his peers live in:

> Most of the young people in Spanish Harlem are bitter and disillusioned. They sit on the stoops because there isn't anything else most of them can do, and they play cards and they joke. "Our goal is to have a good time, to keep having fun so we don't have to think . . ." You know what we're doing? We think we're sending the world on its own way while we go on ours. But we know, and man, that's the trouble, we know that we can't send the world away, that we're part of the world and the world is looking down at us and snarling and laughing at us.[1]

Yet the pain that that truth could inflict on any teacher working in a classroom with such minority groups is easily side-stepped. It's simple enough to dip into another American bag of stereotypes and come up with the comfortable one, "Oh, they're just fun-loving kids. They don't really care about books or ideas." And Shazam, he doesn't have to teach them, only keep them quiet. He doesn't have to devise materials fashioned to draw them out of the bitterness; all he has to do is force-feed them materials prescribed for whites and developed by middle-class white administrators. Indeed, there must be a hundred other ways to get off the hook of responsibility to our constituents.

In short, our curriculum has much to do with students tuning out and dropping out. And most students are rightly convinced *a priori* that the materials of a classroom fall in a special category. That what is used there will not have the tempo, the treble, nor the immediacy of what happens outside.

Those prejudices are deeply ingrained for they were no doubt bred by elementary and preschool experiences. And it is only after they are acknowledged and used as partial guides for the rejecting and the selecting of materials for the classroom that we can even begin to spark our students' thinking and creativity.

It would seem that most of us have no quarrel with the conception of today's young people as children of the McLuhan Age. Why then is there so little tapping of the experiential richness implied by that observation? Is it because we are afraid of change? of innovation? of listening to the ideas which our students have about their world and about themselves?

Certainly there is no one way to go about utilizing the high schooler's world in his education. The goal is not a new one (although our rhetoric may be); some routes to it have already been charted.

There is, for example, a fine periodical geared to assist the teacher in making the transition between pop culture and academia. The magazine is *Media and Methods*. In a recent issue the film *Charly* was discussed and detailed comparisons made between its form and effect as film, short story, and novel. *Charly* was a film which appealed to high schoolers; in a classroom the title would be familiar to most and the plot and characterizations would be familiar to some. This kind of overlap between what students do outside of school and what is talked about in class is important. For the teacher is actually converting an enjoyable experience into material for a deeper learning experience and in doing so bringing the vitality and glamour of the out-of-class world into the school.

Viewed differently, the teacher, in the language of Buckminster Fuller, is tapping the experiential inventory of the student.

A number of things may be accomplished by doing this. First, the teacher may be opening up new avenues of interpretation to the student in those very materials which he already has feelings and thoughts about. Second, the teacher may be legitimatizing the student's out-of-school experience in a new way. Not that he needs your approbation—his peer group takes care of much of that—but there is a significant and qualitative difference when a role model, or a substitute parent, says, "Yes, that film has value for us here too." Third, the teacher is relating *himself* to the student. That is usually not what we mean by achieving relevance, but it's about time we meant that.

Today when we speak of relevance, and I cannot remember a time when it has been spoken of more in educational circles, we're usually talking about materials for minority group students and we generally mean, "use of materials which reflect the student's own experience." I'm afraid that this means picking up Piri Thomas' novel *Down These Mean Streets* if we have Puerto Rican students, Claude Brown's *Manchild in the Promised Land* if we have blacks, or the classic *Laughing Boy* if there are American Indians in our classes.

There are several problems with this smorgasbord approach, but I'll look at only one. This technique simply does not take into consideration class differences which may be more divisive in a classroom than the racial differences. What daughter of a well-to-do Puerto Rican restaurateur is going to identify with the street life which scars and shapes the life of the dark-skinned Piri Thomas? What child of a middle-class black family can recognize himself in the small, fundamentalist church which is central in Baldwin's *Go Tell It on the Mountain?* In other words we need to do more than supply our students with books which are peopled with dark characters. We cannot blithely assume that they will find themselves among the pages.

Let me be clear in my position. Materials with dark characters should be used in classrooms. However, they must be carefully selected and just as carefully handled in a class. I would guess that a teacher might well be merely supplanting one stereotype with another if he were to use *Down These Mean Streets* as the example of Puerto Rican life. How much richer the learning experience could be if students were to contrast the nature of the street life in that novel with that in Claude Brown's and to note the absence of such in Baldwin's.

Also, one underlying assumption of this cafeteria approach is that the relevance of minority materials lies principally in the particularity depicted. The logical extension of that thinking would exempt all-white classes from exposure to such materials. *Invisible Man* and *Raisin in the Sun* give the lie to that narrow view, for such works, while they have dark characters, transcend race in their truths about the human experience.

So, I am sure that the best kind of relevance draws both upon the student's own experiences and the best of literature, white and black. With the former version we know that this is where the student's at. And we invite him to use his experiences. We ask him to write an essay of comparison between the ritualistic "Perry Mason" and the less predictable and more social-issue oriented "Judd for the Defense." Or we ask him to do an analysis of the lyrics of the Beatles' provocative song, "A Day in the Life."

Or we ask him to discuss the structure or lack of it in the Steve McQueen film *Bullitt*. Or we ask for an essay on the main points of appeal of the comic strip "Mary Worth" or on the militaristic stance that permeates the adventures of "Steve Canyon." There are countless ways of entering the high school student's world. We must do so if we are going to excite his imagination, trigger his thinking, and expand our own consciousness.

If departments of English refuse to make themselves relevant, they will be washed into some stinking backwater of academia. I fear that we are not far from that catastrophe now: the National Study for the Teaching of English in the Junior Colleges reports that the demand for English teachers in two-year colleges in 1979 will be 360 times greater than the supply.

The difficulty of attracting to the study of language and literature students who are live, questioning, and exciting will be worsened unless we give life and reality to the term *relevance*. We will find increasingly that those students who want to investigate real issues will be seduced—to some or to little purpose—into departments of social science. And our departments will remain the safe fortresses within which the dreamers and the escapists can find refuge from the strains and cries of the real world.

In saying this, I am not opting for the conversion of English classes into ones in which sociology texts predominate. I am, however, raising the question of whether techniques such as essay writing in class or assignment of research papers, the traditional assignments of the high school English teacher, aren't being used to calcify out-of-date images of the student and the world he moves in. They could so easily be turned into devices which could assist the student in seeing himself and his environment in terms which are meaningful to him.

Why, for example, should a student be assigned a subject to research for three to six weeks? Isn't it conceivable that the student has ideas about something he wants to investigate? Perhaps it's the evolution of rock and roll, or the history of draft resistance or the psychological explanations for the increased popularity of drag racing.

Too, it's quite possible that some student of this electronic generation may be more comfortable using tapes than the typewriter in reporting his findings. The teacher who is persuaded of the rightness of implanting the shape and form of the footnote permanently in the student's soul and mind will not find this a feasible alternative. But the one who is willing to let a student explore a virgin route to the wealth and riches of the library will permit this and other kinds of experimentation.

And even that old essay chestnut, "What I Did on My Summer Vacation," can be modified in a promising way. Changed to "What I Wish I Had Done on My Summer Vacation," it invites the student to draw upon the emotional reservoirs of frustration, fantasy, or fancy. The other is a mere exercise in reportage. Other essay topics which range about the subjunctive mood should be used, for they ask the student to be inventive and to spin out original visions of his selfhood, his peers, and his larger world.

The simple device of offering the student a choice of two or three topics, while it can deplete the teacher's repertoire rather quickly, is immediately less stifling than the practice of foisting one topic on twenty-five different minds. In short, there are some slight modifications that can easily be made which will admit more air and light into the classroom.

Now, let's take a rapid and giant step to a broader social plane. I want to make some observations there which I believe have a macrocosmic relationship to the nature of change in the high school setting. I both witness and suffer the uncountable gross and petty instances of discrimination which black people are daily subjected to in this land. I have never been solaced by the comment of the sympathetic white who says, "I know how you feel and I am so sorry that happens." I usually don't bother to tell him that he really does not know; he only thinks he does.

But more and more Americans, white Americans, are getting to know what discriminatory acts feel like and how the weight of repression hurts. For the social scene in America is changing, rapidly and regrettably. The corporate repressiveness is leaking over the ghetto walls and is affecting the lives of nonblack Americans, both the well-intentioned and those who consciously pin the powerless under their heels.

Some examples: A speaker's ban at the University of Mississippi designed to bar controversial black speakers is protested by white collegians because it also locks out an outspoken white politician they want to hear. And a police force in Chicago which has busted black heads with impunity, having found the feel of flesh sweet against their clubs, fails to take note of skin color after a dangerous while and swings wildly on August nights at blonds and brunets. Tear gas sprayed in Berkeley interferes with the sleep of little children who cannot even spell *People's Park*. Because you did not cry out, because you did not oppose the denial of others' rights, you are gradually losing your own.

And I think a similar process has happened on our high school campuses. Most teachers have never questioned the legitimacy of the power base they straddle as they tower in sometimes dictatorial fashion over their students. And it is dictatorial because they demand this and demand that, rarely asking what it is the students want. Never asking what interests them and often not doing what is in their own best interests.

And it is this posture which has made teachers vulnerable. For they have had their own rights and privileges eaten away as they have kept eyes trained on the student lest he overstep some arbitrary line of propriety.

A case in point is that of Roberta Kass, an American history teacher in a suburb of Chicago. She is young, in her early twenties, and although fresh out of graduate school, as a Woodrow Wilson scholar, she has twice been fired. The principal at one high school said she must lengthen her slightly-above-the-knee skirts. She wouldn't; she was relieved of her job.

That was last summer. This year she has been fired from another high school although the chairman of her department said that her teaching showed a natural ability to present things in a meaningful way. She explains, "I was fired because I was relevant—because I didn't recite mere facts and expect the kids to lap them up, and because I allowed them to write a student paper the administration described as 'provocative, profane and sarcastic.'"

Teachers like Roberta Kass have lost their freedom. In this case, and I don't think it is unique, a dress code is extended to the faculty. In another case, a teacher working with students who disputed the exclusive voice of the establishment newspaper and allowed them to publish their own discovered that she had overstepped the boundaries in doing so. It took the threat of action by the American Civil Liberties Union to force the school to consent to the continued publication of the newspaper.

Oddly enough we hear much about the teacher in the ghetto school who is terrorized by the students. Why do we hear so little about the perhaps more subtle ways in which teachers are kept in line in the nonghetto schools, this time not by the students, but by the administration? There is an artful form of intimidation in the proffering of tenure, the assignment of summer school positions, or the recommendations which may grease the route to promotions or increments.

Most teachers are not free to object to the ludicrous and time-wasting practices of high schools, such as requiring passes for passage. Most teachers are not free to experiment with curriculum so that it even begins to keep pace with the tenor and tone of the teenager's life style. Most teachers dare not wear a turtleneck sweater in their own classrooms.

Slowly, however, things are changing. Today, high schoolers

are raising challenges which are basic to human existence. The issue of freedom of speech is raised by the very establishment of the underground newspaper. The issue of taxation—and indeed we often tax our students' patience and good sense with our sometimes irrelevant and out-of-date curriculum—without representation is raised when the students' suggestions about classroom materials or methodology are systematically rejected. The issue of a quite personal freedom is raised when students question a dress code which dictates what they should and should not wear.

With such various and unreasonable strictures placed on the typical high schooler it seems hypocritical of teachers and administrators alike to complain that students do not act alive in the classroom. How long can any creature which has no voice in establishing and little voice in changing its environment manifest vitality?

Who let the students in? We did. And as teachers, as English teachers, we must gracefully begin to share that power we have sometimes tyrannically wielded. As teachers we should be grateful to those students who have shaken off the restrictions and have broken ground for our doing the same in the entire school community.

I believe that American public school education has been pushed to a crossroads. In one direction lies greater repression; in the other lies greater freedom for all of us to express ourselves with a new sense of selfhood within those school walls.

Finally, it is no doubt significant that some of America's most influential black and white thinkers wrote not from her schools, but from her jails. I think of Malcolm X, Eldridge Cleaver, Henry David Thoreau, and Martin Luther King, Jr. What is the atmosphere, what is the freedom that a prison offers that our schools do not? Is it possible that a man is freer to grow and to discover himself in a cell than in a classroom?

---

[1] Reprinted with permission from *The Way It Spozed to Be* by James Herndon. Copyright © 1968 by Simon & Schuster, Inc., New York.

6

English: Liberal Education or Technical Education?

f I may, I would like to begin in a personal vein. I have, like any intelligent student of teaching and learning, gone through a long developmental cycle. During my first two or three years I was, like most teachers, preoccupied with methodology. Then suddenly, almost between two days, I came to see that the great questions in education are questions of purpose and content, with methods in a barely ancillary role—and I became, for life, a curriculum man.

As time wore on I developed less and less respect for content that was there only for reasons of academic respectability or tradition. I came to see that a great deal of it is mere deadwood, inert,

Fred T. Wilhelms/Executive Secretary, ASCD/Presented at the Richmond Institute

worthless, and often worse than worthless. On the other hand, my respect for the time of students and of teachers rose in a steep curve. Every hour of it ought to be spent on what really counts, on what functions to make life different and better. I became, and remain, savagely discontented with timid curricular tinkering. Radical surgery is what it takes.

The ideal I choose to steer by is the ancient and honorable one of liberal education. By this I do not mean a set of calculated dosages of technical training in a group of disciplines that by some intellectual sleight of hand have come to be known as the liberal arts. I mean education which chooses and uses organized subject matter drawn from high in the culture, but chooses and uses it for the paramount purpose of helping each child toward his full potential as a human being.

When I say that the only curriculum content I came to defend is what really counts in life, I find that people tend to translate this into words like *practical* or *utilitarian*. Perhaps I myself so interpreted it for a while. But if I ever did, that was years ago. I still demand a payoff, yes. If we can't honestly expect that for a given youngster a piece of curriculum content will have a significant payoff we ought to have the integrity to quit wasting his time on it. But I do not see the payoff exclusively, or even much, in terms of what is commonly meant by the word *practical*. Neither, by the way, do I see it in terms of its efficacy in getting the student past college boards.

The fundamental question is this: does what we press on a youngster to learn have a reasonable probability of functioning? Will it change his life in desirable ways? Will it change his society in desirable ways?

This is a terribly harsh criterion. It takes a lot of nerve to face up to it. But, for me, it takes even more nerve to admit that we should ask thousands of teachers and millions of students to spend the days of their lives in what we know to be essentially useless pursuits.

When I apply this demanding criterion to the field called English, I come away in sober disappointment. English as we have known it is, I believe, essentially a failure, so bad an investment that it should probably be permitted to wither away. I say this in profound sorrow, for I believe the two broad sets of objectives we have entrusted to the field—those having to do with communication and those having to do with literature—rank at the very top of any sensitive educational scale. But by and large both have been debased into exercises in technical virtuosity irrelevant to the real lives of real people.

On the side of the language arts, which for purposes of shorthand I shall simply call composition, our overriding purpose has been an antiseptic sort of correctness. I know that recent developments in linguistics have loosened up a lot of rigidities, but is it not still true that the basic medium of instruction remains the writing of largely artificial themes? And if we look at what a typical teacher does with those themes, will it not still be true that most of her red ink goes to formalities? How many teachers pause first to emphasize the ideas expressed? And how many, even of those, give sympathetic attention to the feelings of the student that made him say what he said?

I suspect that in ten or twelve years of such instruction we succeed, by a host of subtle means, in teaching a student that what he has to say and why he cares to say it are of little importance, but whether he says it in correct form is paramount. I suspect that in the process we contribute far more to the rigid and closed personality than to the open and communicative one.

Now if this is true—or in whatever degree it is true—it is in direct contradiction to everything that good speech and writing stand for. Every author whose work has any authenticity puts maximum stress on plumbing his own feelings and ideas and then hewing them out with the utmost clarity and openness, regardless of where the chips fall. The first hallmark of the good speaker or writer is self-respect: respect for his own impulses and thoughts. The second is a willingness to expose himself by expressing himself.

Likewise, if it is true that we drive youngsters into rigid, self-concealing noncommunication, we are committing a crime against their development as human persons. One of the great needs of our humanity is for sensitive, open communication from the center of one person to the center of another. Our young generation, particularly the much-ridiculed flower children, have sensed this and have gone to great, sometimes bizarre, lengths to achieve it. Our psychologists hold it as one of their highest purposes. They speak of transparency and congruence, and exercise all their ingenuity to open people up. The movement for sensitivity training is accelerating at a great rate. Business is spending large sums to help its executives reach out toward genuine communication.

And we in the schools? By and large we still hack along, correcting papers and speeches. I am driven to the conclusion that no mere tinkering with methodology will help very much. The basic theme-writing, report-making bit, with all its artificialities and formal restraints, is essentially maladaptive, sterile but worse than sterile, actually hostile to real communication. It just needs to be jettisoned, and we need a wholly new setting.

Turning now to the side of English which involves literature, I am forced to start with the bitter premise that we drive more children away from a valid use of literature as a life-resource than we attract to it. We may not damage significantly those youngsters who in their home environments have already taken to literature. We may bore them, but we may also help them in technical ways. Anyway, they will go on. But most of the others we stop cold in their tracks. Literature is not part of their lives. They may never have seen either parent read a book. When, then, the first samples they encounter turn out to be, for them, dull, boring, meaningless, and incomprehensible, that's it, brother! They go away and probably never come back.

What a waste! What sheer, unmitigated tragedy! Here we sit, with the greatest life-forming resources that mankind owns, and we reduce them to pieces of pedantic ritual. For what? How could we have gone so wrong?

I believe we lost our way when we forgot what literature is for. We forgot that no poet or dramatist or novelist is long away from the aching problems of the lonely human soul or the jarring dissonances of a sleazy society. We forgot that literature is the great treasure chest of intuitive perceptions of human nature with all its irrational impulses, its amiable follies, and its godlike aspirations. We forgot that books have moved men and whole societies to new levels of ethical values and to new sensitivities on the relation of man to man. We forgot that in literature we had the world's greatest resource to help each youth understand himself and others, refine his values and aspirations, and form a lasting commitment to life on the high road.

Having forgotten all this, we organized a generations-long insult to authors and artists and composers. We behaved as if they had sweated out their lives to produce pretty specimens of prose and poetry, of intricate plot, and of mystical symbolism. We behaved as if what young people need is to know about literature, about the biographies of writers, about the periods of realism and romanticism, about the niceties of rhyme and rhythm. We cultivated what the Romans called *nasum rhinocerotis*, the nose of the rhinoceros; as if to sniff at a work to see whether it is great is somehow better than to simply let it do its work in us. And all too often we reduced all this to the pendantic dissection of a small list of things called *classics*, generally called that by no one but schoolteachers and not read even by them.

And what a selection we made! Like the Latinists who, with all the Roman literature at their command, chose Caesar's *Gallic Wars* because Caesar had a nice prose style—and never mind the immorality of subtly backing a series of raw, unprovoked military aggressions against decent, innocent peoples—like those Latinists we chose our *Silas Marners.*

Now I know, and I am wonderfully glad to know, that English education is opening up, that we are moving to the use of more teaching materials, better and more relevant materials, and a tendency toward free reading. But I also know that *Silas Marner* is still in there as one of the two most widely used classics, that the whole paraphernalia of required readings, *explication du texte*, and book reports is still pretty dominant. More important, I sense that the chief drive is still to get children to know about certain authors and works rather than to internalize them. And I am forced to estimate that in anything like the present context the old preoccupations have so hopelessly firm a grip on teachers' minds that the only thing to do is junk the system.

And then what? I pin my hopes on the new movement toward the unified humanities. As you know, in the incredibly short period of five to ten years several thousand American high schools have launched unified humanities programs in an endless variety of designs. They are still grossly inadequate. Mostly they are one-year courses, generally for seniors, and often only for the brighter seniors, as if the rest weren't human enough to need the humanities. Generally, they are an effort to achieve a synthesis of the arts, music, and literature, though some move well beyond this. All too often, I fear, they are falling into the trap of a pretentious, intellectualized aestheticism, as if aesthetics is all there is to the humanities.

And yet I very humbly salute the pioneers who are spading out these new programs. For I believe they are doing something far greater than just introducing a new course, better even than producing a powerful new synthesis of the arts and literature, valuable as that is in itself. At their best they are genuinely striving for what they often call *a study of man*. And in doing this, I believe they are responding with profound intuition to the greatest need of our time.

We are living in one of those periods in the history of mankind when suddenly things go to pieces. As John Donne wrote, " 'Tis all in peeces, all cohaerence gone, All just supply and all Relation." People are all torn up, not only youth, though perhaps especially youth. There is too much change to be assimilated. Doubts and hostilities arise. Old institutions and old values crumble before the new ones are grown.

So today our youth are restive, many of them alienated, lost in anomie, doubting the very significance of life. Robert Havighurst, that dean of students of adolescence, estimates that in the top half of our student bodies one-third of the young people have not found anything to which they can commit themselves. And any fool can see that in the lower half—and especially in the minority groups—sullen, sometimes explosive anger and disgust are rampant. Rightly or wrongly, millions of our youth find no satisfactions in the old religions and no comfort in the social system.

Their behavior is sometimes bizarre and often annoying. In some groups it merges easily into violence, and in others into dangerous experiment with drugs or sex or sheer oddity. It is easy to lampoon the long hair and the weird clothes and all that. It is easy to criticize the lack of rationality and the absence of constructive alternatives. For in all truth the most vehement protesters seem to have little that is constructive to offer.

And yet, to me, the salient fact is that they are searching. Underneath all their bumptiousness, I see them as the most idealistic generation I have ever known of. They have the nerve to call a spade a spade and to take on our most powerful institutions. Many of them see the values our society actually lives by as sleazy and the values it professes as phony. If they bother us, we bother them far more. They are on the warpath for something better. And I hope they don't give up.

Yet I also see them as badly in need of help. Their lashing out is frequently futile. They don't know where to look for that elusive something better. They need help and they deserve it. But adults mostly just sit around being judgmental; parents are scared—with good reason; and the typical faculty just wrings its hands in helpless dismay.

Well, we are not all that helpless. We have tremendous resources, and the time is right for a great new drive. Suppose we were to join these restive youth in their great quest for superior values, a better relation of man to man and man to himself, a finer society. We could not wish for better resources than we have right here in the humanities.

Only—if that really is what we are talking about, if we really mean to mobilize an authentic study of man, if we mean to help each youngster understand and accept himself and others, if we mean to give him opportunity to refine his values and form a great moral commitment—then we are no longer talking about the kinds of humanities programs we are now forming. For one thing, we are no longer talking about a one-year course; it has to be a great stream running at least through the six secondary years, but really also from kindergarten on into college and serving all the kids. For the sort of inner growth we desire is the slowest of all human events. Neither are we talking any longer about the pretty sort of intellectualized aestheticism that we used to call *culture*. Our purpose will be only incidentally to teach about literature and the arts. Our real purpose will be to use these powerful resources to help young human beings form themselves. That is a very different thing.

Furthermore, literature and the arts won't be subject matter enough. Shakespeare was a great intuitive psychologist. Ibsen was a great intuitive social critic. But we have more than intuitions available now. This is the century of the behavioral sciences, and we ought to be literally ashamed of not using them. The humanities will have to reach out to psychology to help youngsters understand and accept their unconscious and irrational impulsive life. They will have to reach out to social anthropology to help youngsters examine social mores and value conflicts in a way they can handle. Philosophy will be in their domain, too, and so will sociology.

You see, I am not proposing some slight change in subject matter or its organization. I am proposing a basic change of purpose. I believe it is imperative that schools dedicate a sizable block of time—say about one-fourth of the day—to a deliberate attempt to help each young person in his personal becoming.

To do this we must forbid ourselves to start with any body of subject matter. We shall need subject matter, of course, but that can come later. First, we must push ourselves unremittingly to get our purposes clear. Then, when we know what we want to do, we can start casting about for subject matter that has a chance of doing the job. Only in the humanities are we still wholly free to do this. Everything else has syllabi, state requirements, college entrance examinations—and a long, dragging tail of tradition.

In this brief period of freedom, then, before humanities programs also take a rigid set, what do we wish to do? Suppose we were a secondary faculty team, free to invent a six-year program, what would it be like? It will take a great many minds and much experience to begin to answer that. Still, I'd like to suggest a crude sketch. Maybe the best way to get at it will be to dream a little.

Odd though it is, let's start with facilities. Suppose that somewhere in your building there was a "humanities lab." A series of rooms, really—a suite— for you'd likely want spaces where kids could fool around a bit with painting or sculpture or simple music making; but one big central room that would have the sunny feel of a good library, with alcoves for small groups to talk in. Only, this library would also have high-fidelity stereo recordings of the world's great music (great by various criteria, including those of the youngsters) and first-rate playback equipment (with head-

phones, so one or a few could listen without bothering the class).
Similarly it would have, in transparencies and/or paper, a wide
range of fine art (again, fine by criteria that include those of the
learners) and desk-top projection equipment. It would have book
review supplements and drama sections from newspapers, to make
this season's happenings in the world of books and dance and
theatre seem like the exciting events they are. From here on, teachers may furnish the lab as they like, except that I'll insist on deep,
comfortable, homey chairs. (Is this frightening, my asking for an
environment suited to the humanities? Why? Teachers are used to
expensive science labs. Does English always have to be the cheapest
subject there is?)

Then suppose we had a varied staff, not necessarily all present
on any one day or even in any one semester, but all part of a team,
for planning, for sharing, for teaching: literary specialists, of course,
with some variety among them; musicians, some of whom dig the
current thing; artistic people, reaching out into architecture and
over into Africa and the Orient, and not scared of graffiti; a psychologist or two, and at least one cultural anthropologist, and
maybe other behavioral scientists. (Is this frightening, my asking
for behavioral and social scientists as well as sensitive people from
the aesthetic fields? Well, it will be a big stretch across divergent
disciplines. But, remember, we're after a study of man, not a study
about the arts and literature.)

Then, and here we really have to dream, suppose this team had
nerve enough to go into the classroom with only the barest out-
lines of any structure; with a structure so open they could go almost
anywhere within it. No preset list of books to read, composers to
know, and all that; just a serene confidence that as they got into
their investigation of man they could find the right things, for the
group or for individuals. An emergent curriculum.

Now take a deep breath and let go for one even farther-out
dream. Suppose we could forget the whole standard mode of teaching, the whole business of assigning, testing, and thought-control.
Suppose, instead, we could capture the ease and leisureliness of a
good after-dinner conversation. Suppose the youngsters were free
to read around, listen, dabble, reflect. Suppose we could join with
them, or not join with them, in endless talk about what they were

reading, learning, seeing—about what it meant to them. We could help sharpen their talk about values; we could help them hammer out their own great commitments; once in a while we could even organize a field for them. But we could not do the basic job for them.

I believe this because I believe that the humanities are like nothing else in the curriculum and need to be taught in a wholly new spirit and mode. Knowing about some books, authors, movements, etc., has its values, but it is not the central thing. Books, music, art do their wonderful work within us only when we soak in them relaxedly, with all our pores open. Didacticism can be counterproductive.

Besides, it is unnecessary. Every human being is constantly striving to make himself more adequate. Consciously or not, he is trying for new insights into life, for a sense of himself and his significance, for purpose and a mission. If we help a student get in touch with what has meaning for him, on his own terms, he will largely do the rest.

I do not claim that even the best humanities program will do the whole job of rescuing lost, alienated youth, and helping them hit their stride into life. I only know that the humanities are the best medium we have. And finally I know that it is time for schools to free some significant part of their time and work from fact-mongering and technicalities, time for every school to dedicate some part of its every day to a deliberate attempt to help each young person in his personal becoming, to rise a little closer to the potential he has because he is human.

7

A Language Policy
across the Curriculum

O n April 7, Penguin Books published an education special
called *Language, the Learner and the School*. The book is
concerned with the role of talk in learning, and the last
section consists of a document prepared by the London Association
for the Teaching of English entitled: "A Language Policy across
the Curriculum: A Draft Discussion Document for Schools." We
intended this for staff-room and faculty discussion, i.e., we wanted,
somehow or other, all teachers—not only English teachers—to consider in what ways they, as teachers, are concerned with language
learning in the course of teaching their subjects. In particular we

Nancy Martin/University of London/Presented at the St. Louis
Institute

are asking whose is the overall responsibility for students' language development.

Let me begin by outlining the situation in which the need for a language policy across the curriculum has become apparent. In Britain, as in the United States, an increasing number of secondary schools are starting programmes which in one way or another are attempts at curriculum reform. Some schools are unstreaming their junior classes which implies an increase in group methods of teaching; others are attempting to integrate work in groups of subjects, such as English and social studies, by allotting blocks of time and providing team teaching, resources, and space for group and individual assignments. There are many variations but most of them have in common the intention of finding areas of study which the pupils will see as relevant to themselves.

The background of these attempts at reform is, of course, the massive dropout of pupils at fifteen. The bald fact is that the majority of our pupils leave school without the ability or the wish to proceed with any further education—and for their last two years in school, many of them have been making steady progress in failure.

In most of these curriculum experiments English figures as a contributing subject, but over and above English as a contributing subject, there is a strong case for looking at the overall language picture presented by the curriculum as a whole. The relationship of language learning (mother tongue) to learning in general has been a persistent thread in educational enquiry in Britain and the United States for some years now; and although we know that language is learned by encountering it, there has been no serious attempt to survey the kinds of language that children meet and use in their school environment, and in particular the kinds of language through which the traditional secondary school curriculum is taught. Neither has there been any attempt to see the extended uses of language implied in experimental programmes as a key tool in reform.

Why is this? I think it is because such a survey and such a view of the role of language and learning cuts across the traditional structure of our curricula. It demands the contributory thinking and the active cooperation of teachers of all subjects, yet the whole structure of our education system inhibits this. Are there, for instance, teachers of subjects other than English at this conference of the National Council of Teachers of English? And I doubt if there will be any at our national conference now taking place at Manchester. The fragmented pattern of much secondary school education means that most teachers are concerned only with their particular bit of the total picture. And only those who design the curriculum and make the time table are in a position to review the whole operation, and usually these are chiefly concerned to make some sort of reasonable fit out of all the conflicting demands for time, space, equipment, etc. It is taken for granted that the kinds of language learning that go with the various subjects is the responsibility of the teachers concerned, and that teachers of English ought, but often refuse, to be responsible for some sort of general standard of acceptability in written English. (Spelling, punctuation, grammar, and all that). This is a kind of folk view of language teaching, and in this situation, the potential that lies in the relationship between language and learning goes unnoticed. To put the problem rather crudely; those who design curricula and time tables and most of those who operate them do not see a systematic language policy as a part of curriculum reform, while those who do see this —teachers of English in the main—are not in a position to plan or carry out an overall policy.

The working out of such a policy would need to be rooted in a theoretical understanding of how the mother tongue is learnt and of the part it plays in individual development. Who has such an understanding? On the one hand teachers and administrators do not give much thought to the role of language in learning; on the other, linguists do not think much in practical terms about the overall needs of school pupils. In fact, in England it is from teachers of English as a mother tongue that work is beginning to come which will enable the planning of different school curricula to include an appropriate language policy.

About 1000 copies of the discussion document have seeped their way into schools by means of our members. Where the staffs talk to each other and have meetings, reception has been good. But it has also been met with hostility and apathy—and what emerges sharply is that our members do not have a good enough theoretical knowledge of the relation of language to learning. Consider, for instance, what little data we have with its focus on the role of the mother tongue in learning. It is true that much work has been done, particularly in the United States, on children's acquisition of language; the structural language patterns that children use; basic vocabulary; the language level of children of different social groups. All sorts of experimental attempts have been made to improve children's language skills, and much work has been done on the social functions of speech. But where are the surveys and detailed analyses of the actual language that children meet and use in school?

I suggest that we need to know in detail what the language that children encounter in the classroom is like and how the encounters with their teacher's language assist or hinder their learning. We need to know to what extent the talk that goes on among the students in the context of school is an aid to their learning: and we need to know in detail how their writing abilities develop under the influence of the whole curriculum.

Clearly, any interpretation of the data would be made in the light of one's assumptions; for instance, medieval education assigned very different values to reading and writing. The teaching of reading was the responsibility of the church, but the teaching of writing —or penmanship—was regarded as a menial, journeyman task carried out by miscellaneous secular sources; whereas in England today, writing is regarded as a major feature of general literacy and, in broad terms, central to individual development. Therefore, in describing to you the work that is beginning to be done in England in these areas—classroom language, group talk and the development of writing abilities within the context of school, I must also make clear the notions, the theoretical ideas, which lie behind the work.

We are concerned with the relationships between language and experience. Knowledge may be said to be a structuring of experience, but, as America's George Kelly suggested, people differ from each other in their construing of events, so we should expect to find the student's construction of events different from the teacher's. The problem is how to make these various constructions coincide nearly enough for all parties to understand each other. Put more simply, one might ask "How does one make another person's words one's own?" This is really the whole subject of my paper.

I want to make three theoretical points. First, we know that language is the chief means by which we structure experience. Sapir says that language comes to us early and piecemeal in the context of living so that all our experience is saturated with verbalism. So even those symbolic systems which help us to structure experience and which lie outside language have been abstracted from experience which is itself organized by language.

Second, language is learned in our homes and social groups, and we know that different social groups have different life styles and different life styles select different parts of the environment as relevant. For many of our children education has little realized relevance; home is relevant; work is relevant; but in the complex of home/school/work it is school that is out of step. For these children the gap between themselves and school widens with each year, as does the content of the curriculum and the language which goes with it, the language of formal education, and it is formal education which Jerome Bruner suggests chiefly determines the cutoff point in cognitive growth. These children have failed to make the words of their teachers and their textbooks their own. Ernst Cassirer said in his *Essay on Man*, "If I put out the light of my own personal experience I cannot see and I cannot judge the experience of others".

Third, the hypothesis which lies behind our work on the need for a language policy is that the route to the general and the abstract, on which higher education depends, is by means of the personal. New experiences have to be worked over in one's own terms before they can be assimilated, and one's own terms means one's own language, one's own formulation, and this means talk. In school-learning a child's first formulation may be deficient, as is our own when we venture into new ideas, and it is here that real talk with teacher and classmates can provide the occasion for reformulations which will bring the children's understanding nearer to the general. In life we make our own reformulations all the time in our talking. We go over our experiences, retell them; we journey into the future and tell that; we question, and put out a rough dough of ideas and attitudes to be shaped by those we are talking to; we judge and comment, i.e., we work on the verbal representations that others put before us—all this being only a small part of the process of talk.

In what sense is this learning? I suggest that it is the basic process of learning and that it is costly to disregard it. Like all creative activities it is both enjoyable and arduous—Think how much of our time we spend doing this for pleasure only!—but it is a very difficult process to study. We have begun to know something about *how* people learn language, but we know very little about how people learn *through* language.

The things I am going to tell you about are some first attempts to look at the language children encounter in school, in speech and in writing, and how their own language interacts with this. The work is limited and tentative and suggests directions of further work rather than conclusions, but these directions have implications for what goes on in school.

We have been working in three areas. In Leeds, Douglas Barnes has been looking at the spoken language of the classroom—the interactions between teacher and students in formal situations. In London, a group of teachers and I have been making and transcribing tapes of small groups of children in grades 4, 5, and 6 talking together, sometimes with an adult and sometimes without; sometimes with a set task and sometimes without, but broadly within the school context. Thirdly, in the University of London Institute of Education, under the direction of James Britton, we are studying the kinds of written language which students encounter and use in the context of *all* their school work, and we are trying to plot their development between the ages of eleven and eighteen, in grades 7 through 12. This beginning work, because of its implications for education right across the curriculum, is described in *Language, the Learner and the School*.

First, then, I want to look at talk, both in the classroom as part of the lesson and between small groups of children. The questions I am asking are: What is this language like? What are its features? Is it like any other speech situation? Can we see a learning process at work? If so, what is being learnt?

Douglas Barnes recorded and transcribed twelve lessons covering mathematics, physics, chemistry, biology, geography, history, English and religious education. The children involved were eleven years old in their first term in secondary school. In his analysis he tried to perceive the links between the teachers' linguistic behaviour and the children's learning. To do this he examined the demands made upon the students under five heads:

1. Questions asked by the teacher
2. Participation demanded of, or allowed to, the students
3. Language used in instruction
4. Language of social control—threats, flattery, anecdote, etc.
5. Relationship of language to other activities and media [1]

These were not independent categories but instruments of analytic convenience. The teachers' questions, for instance, were drawn from the language of social control and from the language of instruction; these were not five separate issues but were more like five different approaches to the same complex of social behaviour. "To change one might be to change all," observed Douglas Barnes, and at this point I would also quote from John Dixon's *Growth through English*, "Changes in the central activities of the English classroom imply changes in the relation of teacher to pupil . . . . and these in turn imply changes at three levels: in the classroom itself, in the English department, and in the school as a whole." [2] [I would refer also to our language policy document. The reports we have had from schools where it has been discussed show that Barnes spoke more truly than he knew.]

I have only time to take up a few points from this work of Barnes and I have selected three which lead into my general thesis, which is *that we need to legislate for the process of making another person's words one's own and that talk is a major element in doing this.*

The points I want to draw your attention to are concerned with the kinds of questions asked by the teachers, with the sequences initiated by the students, and with the language of instruction.

The Teachers' Questions. These were sorted into four classes: factual, reasoning, open questions not calling for reasoning (e.g., What do you know about Homer?), and social. The factual and reasoning questions were further subdivided into open- and closed-ended questions. I have selected three points for you to think about, remembering that these results apply only to these twelve lessons, but even so they are worth thinking about.

1. The three arts lessons showed seventy factual as against seventeen reasoning questions. Does this surprise you? It suggests that these three teachers, whatever their aims, were in fact more concerned with teaching facts than with thinking, and the children were therefore learning this version of these subjects. In all lessons, of course, there are at least two levels of learning going on: the content of the lesson and the expectation about the subject that the students build up as the result of the questions asked and accepted by the teacher.
2. Reasoning questions predominated in the science lessons, but they were chiefly closed-ended questions leading to a predetermined answer.
3. There were hardly any open-ended questions in any lessons except in English.

When I think about these lessons I want to ask first, whether arts lessons should at this level—eleven years of age—be predominantly factual. And second, whether more open-ended questions in both arts and science lessons might not make learning more effective.

Student Initiated Participation. These sequences were defined as those cases in which a student had of his own accord raised a new issue by either an unsolicited question or a statement. There were only twenty of these in the twelve lessons. It is illuminating to see what they were: three requests for information for its own sake, four requests for information to confirm an insight, one request for a theoretical explanation, six questions about the method of carrying out a task, and six statements. Perhaps nine of these sequences show the students engaged in learning as actively as an intelligent adult does. This is so minute a fraction of the total time of the twelve lessons that we ought to think about the matter.

The Language of Instruction. This is the great divide which separates the student's home life and language from his formal education. Let me expatiate on this for a moment. School is the arena in which the student is confronted with verbalised thought on a systematic and ordered basis—the language of theories, analysis, and speculation, but the concepts which make all this possible are embodied in special languages and sublanguages, and language like this looks at children across a chasm. I want to quote here from an article by Harold Rosen on the language of textbooks.

> The worst way to bridge this chasm is to encourage children to take over whole chunks of it as a kind of jargon. For fluent students it is fatally easy, and instead of the new formulations representing hard-won victories of intellectual struggle, or even partial victories, they are not even half-hearted skirmishes. Instead there is empty verbalism, sanctioned utterance and approved dogma; behind them is a void, or a chaos. The personal view is made to seem irrelevant; it is outlawed; the conventions of this language are taken over unthinkingly, lock, stock, and barrel. Language and experience have been torn asunder.
>
> For other students, however, the gap between their own language and the textbook is so great that the textbook is mere noise . . . it is alien both in its conventions and its strategies. The subject never begins to come through; it is another way of life. Though this is not a matter of language alone, language plays a big part. The willing bright student has sufficient language achievement behind him to enable him to mime the textbook, though his hold may be precarious and over-dependent on verbatim memory. At least his morale will be high when he is confronted with new verbal experience. He has done it before; he will do it again. At the other extreme is the student who receives nothing but scrambled messages. He has failed to decode them in the past; he will fail again.[3]

Now let us look at two examples from the classroom which document Harold Rosen's points. (*Language, the Learner and the School*)

1. A short sequence from a biology lesson.

> T. Where does the air go then?
> S. To your lungs, Sir.
> T. Where does it go before it reaches your lungs . . . Paul?
> P. Your windpipe, Sir.
> T. Down the windpipe . . . Now can anyone remember the other word for windpipe?

S. The trachea.

T. The trachea . . . good . . . After it has gone through the trachea where does it go to then? . . . There are a lot of little pipes going into the lungs . . . What are those called? . . . Ian?

I. The bronchii.

T. The bronchii . . . that's the plural . . . What's the singular? What is one of those tubes called? . . . Ann?

A. Bronchus.

T. Bronchus . . . with "us" at the end . . . What does inspiration mean?

This teacher does seem to be concerned with teaching terminology rather than the process of breathing. Certainly this is what the questions must convey to the students.

2. A short sequence from a chemistry lesson

Here the teacher is concerned with the ideas for which the specialist words are needed, and with his students' need to formulate these in terms of their own experience. He is explaining that milk is an example of the suspension of solids in a liquid.

T. You get the white . . . what we call casein . . . that's . . . er . . . protein . . . which is good for you . . . it'll help to build bones . . . and the white is mainly the casein and so it's not actually a solution . . . it's a suspension of very fine particles together with water and various other things which are dissolved in water . . .

S. Sir, at my old school I shook my bottle of milk up and when I looked at it again all the side was covered with . . . er . . . like particles and . . . er . . . could they be the white particles in milk?

S.2. Yes, and gradually they would sediment out, wouldn't they, to the bottom.

S.3. When milk goes very sour though it smells like cheese, doesn't it?

S.4. Well, it is cheese, isn't it, if you leave it long enough?

T. Anyway can we get on. . . . We'll leave a few questions for later.

What happens here is very different from what happens in the first sequence. Instead of the pattern of teacher's question followed by student's reply, we see four unsolicited student's contributions one after the other; clearly these students expect to formulate for themselves their understanding of what their teacher has put before them, and to ask questions about it. Furthermore one can see the different levels of the children's understanding. The first two are with the teacher and are making explicit the concept of suspension of particles in terms of their own experience. The second two have not understood and the teacher then says, "Anyway can we get on. . . ." The teaching process at work is very different from both the factual terminology questions of the previous sequence, and from the traditional leading question in answer to which the above quoted examples would have been regarded as irrelevant.

This last example is not typical in this sample of lessons. You will remember there were only twenty unsolicited contributions from students in twelve lessons. Here are four of them in a short sequence from one lesson.

I have selected these points from this first pilot survey of language and learning in the classroom because they spotlight certain features in these twelve lessons which we think are matters of concern: the focus is strongly on the handing over of ready-made material and inferences to be learned and handed back. The predominance of factual and closed-ended reasoning questions is a clear indicator of this, as are the scarcity of student-initiated sequences and the lack of systematic attempts to get the students to be explicit about the things they are learning. The chasm is not being bridged.

After all, the teaching/learning situation might make us suppose that there would be a lot of questions from the learners to the teachers. Adults together, for instance, or children among other children, do not hesitate to ask questions about what they do not know, but the role the students see themselves playing in these lessons—and I suspect in many, many lessons—is that of a passive recipient rather than an independent learner. Douglas Barnes's study shows the way in which these "non-conversations" build up this expectation of a passive role. Much more is being learned than the content of the lesson, but does the teacher know this is what is being taught? Does he really want this? This is what we are asking in our policy document.

To change this we should probably have to change a lot of things, many of which are outside the area of the curriculum-makers, but if we could get teachers of all subjects to examine the role of language in learning in their particular subjects we should be on the way to some big changes.

I could of course give you examples from British schools which would show a very different picture, but I have seen nothing so dramatically different as the six lessons that I saw at Evanston Township High School. You will know the pattern: teams of teachers with units of time in which to plan and arrange their work as they agree is best, with a focus on seminar work and individual and group assignments. I attended the small classes—6, 7, 8, 10, 12, and 14 students; some of low ability and some of high, and something so different was happening that I still can hardly believe it. It was like a living documentation of John Dixon's book. First, there was no fear; no destructive discipline battles, so the teachers were free to be perceptive human beings, aware of each student and speaking to them as individuals. Second, the students were free to initiate questions, to disagree, to pursue ideas, in short to converse as free adults do. Third, the teachers met to plan and argue and learn from and help each other. Everything I know theoretically about the importance of talk in learning I found demonstrated in these seminars and in the meetings of the teachers themselves. Here was the best kind of university teaching located in a high school. Two things made it happen: the attitudes of the teachers and the students in the small classes, plus the resources centre and I suppose this means money. Later I asked whether similar patterns were operating in other subjects across the whole curriculum. The answer was yes. I wish I had time to tell you about some of them.

Now I must move on to my second area which is our study of group talk, and what I saw at Evanston leads straight into this.

"We teach and teach and they learn and learn; if they didn't we wouldn't," writes James Britton in his study of group talk in *Language, the Learner and the School*, "and as the syllabus grows longer we teach more, but do they learn more? and if we get three lessons a week when we ought to have five, presumably we teach more to the minute than we would otherwise; but do they learn any quicker?" These are quantitative matters and are easier to find out; but the qualitative matters of students becoming wise as well as well-informed, and able to ask questions as well as answer them, i.e., to speculate and theorise, are terribly difficult to find out. So we in the London Association for the Teaching of English (L.A.T.E.) have been trying to think about learning and to look for examples of it as it happens, forgetting teaching altogether for the time being. "If we could be more certain what learning looked like in some at least of its many guises, we might find it easier to monitor our own teaching."

In our studies of 3, 4, 5, or 6 students talking together we have looked at various situations; at students without and with a teacher as a member of the group; at free talk, and talk for a particular purpose, such as exploring a story or a poem with no more specific instruction than "talk about this story as long as you want to and then turn off the tape-recorder"; or translating English sentences into Latin as a group task; or finding and judging alternative theories to explain the result of a science experiment. In other words, we have transcriptions of structured and unstructured talk by groups of students and are attempting to see in what way, if any, they seem to be learning from talk.

I think it is relatively easy to see the importance of talk in problem solving and in performing new mental operations by the agency of one's own attempts to be explicit about it, but there is a great deal of learning that goes on outside the framework of school subjects. We are suggesting that talk is a major element in this learning too, but to perceive it is nearly as difficult as putting salt on a blackbird's tail. Sometimes this free talk takes the form of argument, and sometimes a very different process occurs in which the talkers perform a kind of conversational spiral; they chime in to support each other's opinions and experiences and make a tissue of little narratives which gradually reveal themselves as forming a slow exploration of some topic to which all are contributing in a supportive rather than a dialectic mode. As this is the most widespread and natural mode of conversation and the least likely to be regarded as a learning situation, I have chosen this one to draw your attention to.

The transcript is a thirty-minute conversation among five sixteen-year-old girls from a London comprehensive school. Seventeen minutes of it are printed in *Language, the Learner and the School.* The girls are talking about their homes and their parents. The question we asked ourselves was: Is anything happening to anybody in this talk? Is anybody changing, or laying herself open to change? James Britton comments:

> As the talk rolls on, we see elements of the family situation laid out for inspection. They are not precise elements like "subject" and "passive" and "third person singular", which when properly inspected and handled may come together as a Latin sentence. But they are there: parents are provided with a history—seen as young couples, with no children, free to go out; and as people with a future, old and needing help from those who now need them; and as separate people with separate likes and dislikes, . . . and as human beings capable equally of wise control and rows over silly nothings. Laid out also are the bits of the family jigsaw itself: father, the one who goes out to work; mother, the one who tidies—and is perhaps equally— "the leader"; brothers and sisters; grandparents, the-not-to-be-neglected. And the various ties that link the pieces in various ways together: love, happiness, protection, anger, guilt.
>
> The speakers offer their own evaluations of the behaviour they talk about: . . . But in general it is a sanctioning process that goes on . . .
>
> [As it] moves on it grows in its power to penetrate a topic . . . At its most coherent it takes on the appearance of . . . a group effort at understanding—enable them, that is, to arrive at conclusions they could not have reached alone . . .

We ourselves think that if we are able to perceive the general function of this kind of free, self-directed talk, which has no explicit, practical aim, we shall know a good deal more about the importance of the students' own contributions in more specific situations, such as the searching discussion of the Book of Job which I sat in on with nine senior students at Evanston High School.

The problem is to know how this kind of talk can be legislated for in school. It can go on freely among friends, out of class, or it may seldom happen. I would suggest that this kind of self-directed talk within a group can often result from the reading of literature which in this instance is explicitly regarded as the starting point for the exploration of the students' own experiences and values. In this case the teacher would not intend the talk to be closely focussed on the literature; I think it was Professor Barbara Hardy at Dartmouth who said, "It's a poor teacher of English who won't ever sacrifice the work to the student."

And now my third area—our enquiry into the development of writing abilities at the secondary level (eleven to eighteen years). In our previous research on English composition we found that at sixteen years nearly all students could cope quite adequately with narrative and almost none could cope with argument. This led us to our hypothesis that the development of writing ability lay in the ability to move appropriately from one kind of writing to another, and that the route to the abstract and general required by higher education is via the personal. You will remember my quotation from Cassirer, "If I put out the light of my own personal experience, I cannot see and I cannot judge the experience of others." Thus our task was to survey and classify the kinds of writing that occur in school in all subjects and then to plot the students' ability to move about effectively within these kinds of writing.

You will remember that our study of writing covers all the work done in school, so we are looking at the work of the same students across all their subjects. We have found some curious and disturbing things but as we are only half way through a five year study the facts and figures I may quote are not complete. As with Douglas Barnes's work I have only time to draw your attention to one or two selected items.

Starting with the assumption that a child's early writing will be relatively undifferentiated and rather like written-down speech, we looked at those influences which make the writer direct it in various ways. (Our model here was drawn from work on the spoken language.) Since it was school writing that we were concerned with and all our scripts were writing tasks set by the teachers, we first looked at the effect of the audience on the writing. This gave us a set of categories which we have called a "sense of audience" which moves from the self as audience, through the teacher in various roles, to a wider audience, the peer group, and, with older students, a general public. The teacher as audience seemed to have four roles: (1) Teacher as confidante or trusted adult; (2) Teacher as teacher (The writing was seen as part of an on-going dialogue.); (3) Teacher as subject specialist (Some of the writing of senior students fell into this category.); and (4) Teacher as examiner

(The writing was seen as a test.). In our sample these roles varied not only according to individual teachers but also by subjects.

Some 2000 scripts have now been read by three different readers and allocated to these categories though my figures are based on only 1300. We set them out by subjects in a tentative attempt to see what the overall picture was like with regard to the range of kinds of writing provided by the various subjects. As one might expect, writings for the teacher in the role of trusted adult was a small category. What is significant is that writing of this kind occurred only in English and religious education. The category most like this one we called unknown audience: writer to his public. In English we found some 5 percent, in foreign languages 2 percent (accounted for by critical essays on literature in grades eleven and twelve), and in science and religious education less than 1 percent. The last are two categories of audience writing in which individual thought and self-direction are features, yet they are marked in our subject sample by absence or very low amounts.

By far the greatest number of scripts fell into the category of teacher as examiner: over 75 percent of science, geography and history, over 50 percent of foreign language work, over 30 percent of religious education, and some 20 percent of work in English were in this category.

This means that in the schools in our sample, the greatest amount of writing was the recapitulation of work done in lessons or derived from textbooks or notes. Whatever the cause, and the pressure of the examination system is likely to be a strong factor, the effect is to minimise initiative in thinking and individual directions in work. Furthermore the requirements of answers to tests presupposes limited modes of writing. There is thus little room for experiment either in approach or in writing.

It is worth noting the bearing these results of ours have on the quite different kinds of evidence produced by Douglas Barnes in other schools. They tell a similar story.

I should like to refer here to one of the experiments from Evanston. In their programme for the least able students, called "A Raid on the Inarticulate," they got the students in each grade to keep a journal. They found daily writing became mechanical so they asked the students to write four or five pieces a week on anything arising (or not arising) from their daily living. These produced such interesting writing that the idea of a journal of individual writing was also tried in the top level grades, again with outstanding results. These are commented on by the teacher but not marked. I have read through the twenty-five or so items in one grade-twelve student's journal and found that most of the items come in the category of trusted adult or a writer to his public; just the categories which are absent in writing done in traditional subjects.

The next point I want to make concerns one of our intervention exercises. Part of our study consists in following up over four years all the written work done in all subjects by two classes in five different schools. But in addition, once a term we set a special piece of work ourselves. One of these was an attempt to see what came when the work was not done for the teacher, so we asked each of the research classes to write anything they wanted, to be sent direct to the corresponding class in one of the other schools. Eventually one of the students in each school returned it to us. The effect of writing to a peer-group audience, though an unknown one, produced a crop of writings that were totally different from writings done in school in the course of ordinary work. There was a very great range of kinds of writing: stories, letters, personal experiences, political arguments, poems, theories about life, comments on characters, judgments about school, ideas about education—the lot.

This suggests to us that students are just not getting enough choice because so much of their written work is so closely geared to set topics. Here, once again I feel I should refer to the work at Evanston where in science, for instance, students may choose to work on individual projects, and each week two seminars are held, in which each student who has opted for this kind of work makes a progress report to some twenty of his peers who question and discuss his work with him.

Again I want to say, we must stop being only concerned with our subjects and must look at the overall picture. I think we must talk to our colleagues about this and try to sort out who is responsible for what. We know that language is learnt on the job—so the students are learning the expositional languages of their different subjects in those lessons—and those lessons form perhaps 70 percent to 80 percent of the curriculum. This means that it is crucial for the

English teacher to see his responsibility as an opportunity for using the language of personal experience—which is the language of literature. But all this has to be thrashed out in discussion with other teachers. This is what our language policy document is about.

We hope it will act as a starter to staff-room discussion. We tried to make it provocative, and it appeared condescending and dogmatic! We toned it down, and it appeared wishy-washy. But you have it before you. It is being discussed in various staff rooms in various parts of England. It is arousing both interest and hostility. We are planning a joint English and science teachers' conference on the subject, and my hunch is that teachers will gradually perceive the relevance of this matter to the teaching of their subjects.

---

[1] Reprinted with permission from *Language, the Learner and the School* by Douglas Barnes, James Britton, and Harold Rosen, published by Penguin Books, Ltd., London. Copyright © 1969.

[2] Reprinted with permission from *Growth through English* by John Dixon, published by the National Association for the Teaching of English, Birmingham, England. Copyright © 1967.

[3] Reprinted with permission from *Talking and Writing* by James Britton, published by Methuen & Co., Ltd., London. Copyright © 1966.

8

Toward a Response-Oriented Curriculum in Literature

I n late summer of 1966, some fifty English educators and twenty-five assorted consultants gathered on the beautiful and isolated campus of Dartmouth College to spend a month of "reasoning together" concerning the future of English teaching. What was unusual about the conference was not only its support by the Carnegie Corporation of New York and the NCTE, MLA, and NATE of the United Kingdom, but that the composition of the conference included leading American and British literary critics, creative writers, linguists of various disposition, and specialists in English teaching at virtually all grade levels. Those present ranged from a world famous phonetician from the University of Edinburgh, the head of the department of psychology at the University of

James R. Squire/Ginn and Company/Presented at the Santa Barbara Institute

London, the leading British specialist on George Eliot, the author of one of the most significant critical works of the past decade, the American director of a significant study on university reform, to primary supervisors and classroom teachers from both suburb and slum. To be sure, college and university professors of English predominated, as they have been wont to dominate in recent curricular reform in America, a fact that is especially important to recall in considering the results of the conference. All in all, however, the total group was probably as distinguished as any which has been convened to consider the basic problems.

Even more significant were the processes of deliberation. For four weeks—of reasoning together, living together, arguing together, working in seminar and study group, debating, discussing, reading, reporting—the participants tended to the task at hand. Much has been written of the "conflict in cultures" that emerged at Dartmouth, much more about the recommendations themselves. Two books and six pamphlet publications represent the official products; article after article continues to express minority opinion. Yet out of bruised feelings and brusk attitudes, out of the cauldron of smashed curricular patterns, a very real consensus emerged.

For me, the Dartmouth Seminar was less an end than a beginning—a beginning of a reassessment of my own views on the teaching of English, an awareness of the inevitable consequences of some of my earlier ideas, a sense that somehow, in some ways, American English education had gone astray. I was fortunate to follow the Dartmouth experience with a detailed on-the-site study of English teaching in England, where with the guidance of leading teaching specialists in the United Kingdom and the support of fellow faculty members from the University of Illinois, I was able to compare the teaching of English in pacemaking high schools of England, Scotland, and Wales with teaching I had earlier studied in the United States. Our findings are reported in a publication which has been released by the National Council of Teachers of English,[1] and I do not propose to review them here. But in commenting on the teaching of literature in our schools, three insights emerging from the Dartmouth experience and my later studies in England may help to establish a point of view:

1. Social and emotional learning are as basic to English education as are intellectual goals. After a decade of emphasis on hard
core intellectual and rational processes in our efforts at curriculum
reform, we must look again at emotional and social processes. It
is not enough for young people to read and study Shakespeare.
What is more important is how they feel about Shakespeare after
the reading has been completed.

2. Sequence and continuity in instruction in English will be
found in students' developing processes involving the uses of
language and the responses to literature, not in inert bodies of
literature, language, and rhetoric parcelled out from grade to grade.
"The best preparation for the next grade level," said Wayne Booth
at Dartmouth, "is the best possible experience at the present grade
level." The conventional questions of curricular reform—What is
the literary heritage that children must have? At what level do we
introduce American literature? What elements of criticism do we
cover in grade 9?—are important questions only if English is seen
as the coverage of established content. The Dartmouth conferees
asked rather, How can a student grow in effectiveness in his use
of oral and written language?

3. The imaginative education of boys and girls must be the
major concern of teachers of literature. It is not enough to implant
facts and knowledge about literature and literary study, to teach
skill in reading, to provide time to read without concern for what
is happening to individuals during the process of reading. Concern
with the creative, imaginative response of the learner to life, to
literature, leads inevitably to the questioning of many conventional
programs in schools today. Are we spending too much time on book
and author and tradition, too little on the pupil's own response?
What we need is not a history-centered curriculum in literature, a
structure-centered curriculum, or a genre-centered curriculum.
What is needed is a response-centered curriculum.

With these views in mind then, with the background of experience which came from Dartmouth and England and from subse-
quent reading, I suggest four dimensions of literary response as
particularly important to consider as schools move toward establishing response-centered literary programs in English.

1. *The ultimate purpose of literary education in the secondary schools is to deepen and extend the responses of young people to literature of many kinds.* There are other purposes, of course: to reinforce values and points of view (as in introducing black literature into the curriculum), to transmit important cultural information, to help young people to learn to apply critical terms or to understand certain critical theories. But these are adjunctive or secondary purposes. What is important is that we perceive literature as human experience—both the experience of the writer and the experience of the reader—and know that when it really works, it can have all of the power and impact of life experience itself. The full study of literature involves concern with the work itself, concern with the writer of the work, and concern with the relationship between the reader and the work. The former are the province of the critic and the literary historian; the latter, of the teacher of literature. This is why response to literature rather than literature itself must be our major concern.

2. *Response to literature is not passive but active.* It is largely internalized and it can involve the full play of the human personality—the rational powers, the emotional reactions, the ethical commitments. Alan Purves has completed the most comprehensive modern analysis of the responses of many kinds of readers—critics and scholars as well as school children. Although Purves' report of the full range of reactions is exceedingly complex, he finds most kinds of responses may be classified in four broad areas:

Engagement. The internalized emotional response to a literary work which involves personal commitment and is present even in the reactions of our most mature readers.

Perception. Those responses having to do with the acquisition of meaning, of basic understanding of what a work means or perhaps how it means.

Interpretation. Those generalized responses through which a reader relates a work to a human experience or to other kinds of literary experience.

Evaluation. Those responses in which a reader judges the worth of a literary work in relation either to personal or external criteria.[2]

These dimensions, variously expressed, suggest the full range of response to literature. Yet school programs, if they are assessed from available courses of study, from the end-questions in literary anthologies, or from reports of classroom observers, seem to limit rather than extend the dimensions of response. Too few teachers, and even fewer students, recognize the importance of dealing directly with the dimension of engagement. Almost no attention seems to be directed to the problem of evaluation, and precious little to interpretation in the large sense in which Purves uses the term. Rather, in emphasizing factual knowledge, literal comprehension, or even intrinsic critical analysis, teachers tend to confine our programs and our students to the dimension of perception when they deal with literary response at all. The teaching of skill in reading and of methods of critical analysis are important in and for themselves. Readers must learn how to unlock basic meaning at various levels. But such instruction is only tangential to actual experience in literature itself. Research has amply demonstrated that some of our most able readers, at least those with high scores on standardized reading tests, can be among our most disabled responders. A good many individuals may understand every word in *Hedda Gabler* and still not sense both rationally and emotionally the brooding malevolence of Ibsen's drama, and the way in which the overt symbolism foreshadows Hedda's relentless march to catastrophe. Without some kind of basic affective reaction to the underlying tension in such a literary work, the reader remains unmoved, detached, and largely incapable of any real literary response at all.

3. *Response to literature is highly personal and is dependent to a considerable degree upon the background of experiences in literature and in life that a reader brings to any literary work.* Still, certain kinds of experience seem sufficiently common to the young people in our culture that they are important to consider in choosing and teaching literature in our schools.

Age and maturity, for example, seem to affect the responses of the individual far more than intelligence or reading ability. The accelerated reader and the retarded reader will often like sports stories, juvenile romances, or animal stories at approximately the same time, albeit the advanced fourteen year old may find his satisfaction in George Plimpton's *Paper Lion* while his classmate responds to far more simplistic writing. Similarly, certain works of literature require a maturity that no adolescent can be expected to have. A few advanced readers may understand every word of Synge's *Riders to the Sea,* but few if any will have lived life sufficiently to respond emotionally, not intellectually, to the endless, inevitable waiting for death that controls the contextual cadences against which this small tragedy is enacted.

Sex differences influence response to literature, particularly during early adolescence, as most teachers inevitably discover. Both "boy books" and "girl books" are needed in any classroom.

Social and cultural differences have a unique and uncertain impact on response, albeit I am not certain they do not work largely in highly individualistic ways. It is true that young people in our urban centers today are seeking a relevance in literary content that we have not always provided, but it is far from clear that, aside from reenforcement of attitude and perhaps initial motivation, that literature written by black writers, for example, about the black experience in America has greater impact on the black reader than on the white. What young readers are seeking, I think, is not the superficial relevance of color but the underlying relevance of the human experience. In the long run it may not be the blackness or whiteness of a protagonist or a writer that is essential but his thought and feeling and response to life.

One aspect of our comparative study of American and British schools reenforces and illuminates this point. In an attempt to identify some of the most compelling literary experiences of adolescents in the United Kingdom and in the United States, we questioned many near-graduates on their most significant literary experiences. The titles most frequently mentioned on both sides of the Atlantic were generally similar; *1984* and *Catch 22,* for example, seem to provide important experiences regardless of where an adolescent lives. But there were differences as well. American students, both black and white, caught in the turmoil of the racial revolution, reported interest in titles like *Black Like Me, Cry, the Beloved Country,* and *To Kill a Mockingbird.* British adolescents could not have been less interested. Instead, they substituted a similar kind of book dealing with the working class struggle—*Sons and Lovers* and

Loneliness of the Long Distance Runner. Here surely we see important cultural differences at work. Some books apparently speak primarily to the social and cultural issues; others reflect something more basic in the human condition. But still we must remember that the overall lists were more similar than different and that the one title preferred above all others on both sides of the Atlantic was William Golding's tumultuous tale of adolescence, *Lord of the Flies.*

Above all, teachers need to remember that response to literature is highly personal and that elements of content in a selection can block or facilitate individual reactions. Henry Meckel's analysis of the reactions of some adolescent boys to Hugh Walpole's *Fortitude,* the story of a son's struggle against father and family, showed that such books can awaken such painful personal associations in some readers as to prevent them from entering the literary experience.

Experiences in using books in the classroom and the results of the reading preference studies may help teachers identify selections appropriate for large numbers of young people at a particular age, but we need to provide also for the uniquely personal choices and reactions, perhaps through programs of guided individual reading.

4. *Response to literature can be affected by methods of approach utilized by the teacher within the classroom.* Conferees at Dartmouth were much concerned with teacher approaches. For example, a recent experimental comparison of the responses to literature of adolescent boys in Belgium suggests they are circumscribed almost entirely by the methods of *explication du texte,* largely because their schooling has concentrated on refining such limited expression of response. Yet it is the opening of a multiplicity of appropriate responses rather than restrictiveness which should be our major goal.

Important in the classroom of course is the position of the teacher and his relations with individual readers. Exploration of literature, discovery of ideas and experiences in texts, open-ended discussions (whether structured or informal) seem crucial. Close reading that leads young people to develop awareness of what is said and how it is said contributes importantly to anyone's literary education and is virtually essential if educational programs are to concentrate on literature and the literary experience. But close reading is not and must not be the only methodological staple of the program in literature, and it must be closely related to wide reading.

Expressions of response by the pupils themselves can occur in many forms. Talking about individual works, in both formal and informal ways, affords readers an opportunity to organize and share their cumulative reactions. Other kinds of oral expressions of response need greater attention: recreating the literary experience through interpretive reading, whether by teacher or pupil reader, provides for some interplay of emotion with reason; dramatizing scenes in informal classroom setting, especially important in developing a sense of the uniqueness of drama as genre. Imaginative writing as creative response deserves greater attention in our classrooms. Dialogue, monologue, narrative, poetry, journals, diaries— any one can engage the reader in the process of imaginative response to human experience. Creation or recreation of literary experience or response through mime, role playing, and improvised classroom drama is common throughout the United Kingdom. During my visits there I saw adolescents completely engaged in dramatizing such events as the experiences of medieval pilgrims and players en route to Canterbury, the impact of the Aberfan Welsh coal mining disaster, the story of the Prodigal Son, the assassination of a president, and, at Easter, the Trial, Crucifixion, and Resurrection. The individual approaches that can facilitate engagement with literature are many, but fundamentally they have one attribute in common: they avoid the routine, the mechanical, the overly technical dwelling on knowledge as fact, on critical method as end, on critical theory as ultimate, and they stress instead the active and vital engagement of each individual in reaching to a literary work or a literary experience.

To achieve such purpose, a program in literature almost certainly must have three dimensions: that which relates the individual reader with the individual book; that which provides for small group experiences in literature; and that which provides shared common experiences for the class as a whole. Clearly it is through the guided individual reading which we attempt to find the "right book at the right time" for each of our readers; and clearly, too, such a program must provide time for careful guidance by the teacher, conferences with individual students on the books they are reading, and conversations during which pupils have opportunity to share with others some of the experiences that they are having in literature. The notion that individual reading can be "outside" reading or "collateral" reading, i.e., something adjunctive to or less important than the major strand of literary programs, implies a clear lack of recognition of what a broad program of individual reading can contribute to literary education. Schools are doing much these days to talk about independent study by pupils; yet how much of this independent study has been employed for wide reading in literature? In our comparisons of British and American youth, we found both groups spending about the same amount of time in reading outside of school hours, yet two-thirds of the time of American youngsters was devoted to assigned reading of school assignments. Only one-third of the reading time of British youth was so restricted. Perhaps one of the reasons why we have failed to educate a nation of book readers is that we are so reluctant to give them the opportunity to develop personal reading habits on their own.

Small group experiences with literature are important as well, particularly if we are to provide opportunity for young people to read and react together to books of many kinds. Small seminar-type discussions of particular titles, perhaps led by students rather than the teacher, have been employed with advantage in some experimental schools. Listening to recorded literature, viewing films as literature, reading poetry aloud in informal small group settings—such communal experiences can generate responses of many kinds.

Teacher presentation of a selection accompanied by class discussion or response remains our most widespread approach, and perhaps always will, although much can be done to ensure that the students as well as the teachers have an opportunity to respond. We need to remember, for example, that we must promote engagement as well as understanding and modify our approaches accordingly. More oral reading by the teacher will help in some classes, and emphasis on the oral is crucial in teaching poetry and drama. Opportunity for young people to formulate their reactions prior to discussion needs greater emphasis too—perhaps a few moments of free talk or free writing after reading is completed or a chance to respond graphically through color and linear symbolism for those less verbally inclined. Such expressions of response, if they precede any organized discussion or questioning, will help some young readers identify their own feelings and ideas. Dramatization can also help. Some time ago, partially as a result of the Springfield Institute, a group of young eighth graders dramatically enacted in class the experience of two hijacked flights to Cuba, with each student assuming the role of a passenger attempting to dissuade the hijacker. The activity, an epilogue to the reading of an essay, was prologue to writing which in itself led to another literary experience. Listening to a recording of a similar or contrasting selection, reading two pieces for comparative purposes, beginning and building on the students' most vivid immediate reactions—these can help project many into active reaction to the piece. The approaches are limited only by the imagination of the teacher and the more clearly in the beginning they can approach the actual reactions of student readers, the greater the impact they are likely to have.

The conferees at Dartmouth said it well:

> Response is a word that reminds the teacher that the experience of art is a thing of our own making, an activity in which we are our own interpretive artist. The dryness of schematic analysis of imagery, symbols, myths, structural relations, *et al.*, should be avoided passionately at school and often at college. It is literature, not literary criticism, which is the subject. At the present time, there is too much learning about literature in place of discriminating enjoyment, and many students arrive at and leave universities with an unprofitable distrust of their personal experiences to literature. At the university, as in the secondary school, the explicit analysis of literature should be limited to the *least* required to get an understanding of the work, within the student's limits, and the aim should be to return as soon as possible to a direct response to the text.

---

[1] *Teaching English in the United Kingdom,* A Comparative Study. James R. Squire and Roger K. Applebee. Champaign, Illinois: National Council of Teachers of English, 1969.

[2] Alan C. Purves with Victoria Rippere. *Elements of Writing about a Literary Work: A Study of Response to Literature.* Champaign, Illinois: National Council of Teachers of English, 1968.

9

Responsibilities and Structures

This is a rather tendentious title, chosen deliberately as a gesture of self-justification and to serve to reassure you that I'm really a solid reliable respectable citizen, since I gather that some strands of English teachers' folklore have it that Dartmouth was a conspiracy on behalf of irresponsibility and the demolition of all structures. Such things couldn't, of course, happen at Dartmouth—it's far too sober an ambience: the very symmetries of its architecture operate powerfully on the subconscious in favour of equilibrium, piety, and conventional wisdom.

Let's clear the ground before we go any further: I want to speak as an elementary school teacher, which is what I have been for 90 percent of the past six months and for 10 percent of the past six

Geoffrey Summerfield/University of York/Presented at the Springfield Institute

years. And I want to speak, more narrowly, as a teacher in a school frequented by poor children—whites, blacks, Spanish-Americans, and Indians. For the purposes of my present argument, I shall assume that the students from middle class or upwardly mobile skilled workers' homes—that *these* students will achieve according to their parents' expectations, will gain entree to the campuses, whatever their schools may do to bore them on their way thither. A rather facile assumption, but please indulge it for the time being.

At the adult level, one meets injunctions that read "Fight Poverty the American Way: Go to Work"; at the students' level, both at high school and at elementary school, the equivalent form of this demonstration of the power of positive thinking would, I suppose, be: "Stave off poverty the American way, by putting your nose into your books, by achieving, and by working for the one reward of achievement." In England we have a simple short way of managing the child's sense, his expectations of possible achievement. If he is a poor achiever or a nonachiever at the age of seven or eight, he is labelled as such; he is then thrust into the C or D stream (the third or fourth track down from the top) and there he tends to stay: exemplification of Pygmalion in the classroom. Such is true of about 50 percent of our elementary and high school classrooms: and in such rooms certain general significant collocations tend to manifest themselves. Such schools—and every other school is such a school— such schools depend heavily on prescribed courses, on textbook English, on clearly defined hierarchies, on a masterful discipline, on the severest interpretation of the reality principle.

What the children tend to do in such a situation is to work through comprehension exercises, to define parts of speech, to develop a nervous tic about apostrophes, commas, and paragraph structures. At the wave of a paddle, they will grope desperately for a topic sentence or try crudely and clumsily to disembowel a clause. The nice kids, the kids who come to school with a clean handkerchief and a full stomach, learn the rules of the game and leap through the hoop or salivate, couthly, at the appropriate signal. But the children that I want to attend to, the not-so-nice, not-so-couth, children: they sink deeper into a morass of mystification, confusion, torpor, and distaste.

The responsibility of the school is not toward them, except to ensure that they stay in the building between 9:00 and 4:00 and, preferably, leave it without trying to burn it down. And the structures, the cognitive structures—exercises in comma disposition leading inexorably upward to exercises in semicolon manipulation— such structures have nothing to do with their ways of proceeding, their ways of ordering experience, their ways of exploring their environment, their ways of being or of trying to become articulate.

Such ways of proceeding are divisive, depressing, and self-defeating. We know little enough of the psycho-pathology of teaching —God knows, we need to know much more—but I'd hazard the guess that the textbook-based courses are more generally used by teachers without vivacity, without natural zest and gaiety, without lively, ironic humour: teachers who need the reassurance of Holy Writ, who are themselves insecure in their judgment, and who probably derive much stress from anal compulsions which many of our schools have institutionalized. So, if the title of this conference has any meaning, "After Dartmouth" will in some contexts take the form of a despairing slump of the shoulders. In California, for example, some of the most enthusiastic and committed young teachers I have ever met are being shifted by insecure principals and chairmen of departments who insist with a peculiar kind of desperation or fanaticism that the students' experience of English must be circumscribed by the front and back covers of the appropriate volume of the Roberts English Series. And the Roberts English Series, let's face it, is really quite dreadful. It puts the clock back not years but decades: it's teaching kids to loathe poetry because every poem that is actually let in is immediately followed by a series of grammatical homilies and questions. It is perpetuating one of the peculiar ills of our society—the sharp dichotomy between reality and pretense—between, say, the strip cartoon or the movie that we genuinely enjoy, and that strange junk called poetry-with-grammatical-and-comprehension-exercises that we are supposed to enjoy: between Longfellow or Jane Austen, that we grind through in grade ten with the help of Cliff's Notes and the buzzing real world of soul, of progressive rock, of Dylan, of electronic music, of concrete poetry, of *Hair,* of Philip Roth, of John Updike, and so on. So: "After Dartmouth", much perpetuation of hypocrisy, of cant, of switchings-off, of tedium, of inarticulacy. And if you think I'm exaggerating visit Lincoln, Nebraska, and observe the sharp discrepancy between the essays written by freshmen in English on respectably literary topics, essays replete with the jargon, the nervous intellectual tics of the literary critics—between the borrowed voice on the one hand and the fumbling stumbling inarticulate thrashing around of the students speaking with their own voices in seminar. The wide discrepancy between the borrowed, the official, and the personal, the unofficial, is one of the peculiar and distressing legacies of our continuing orthodoxies. I'd like to dwell for a moment on just one aspect of the continuing orthodoxy. In *Let Us Now Praise Famous Men* the late-lamented James Agee spoke eloquently of the power of art. Put your ear, he suggested, right up against the loudspeaker and listen, really listen, to Beethoven or Schubert. The result, he insisted, is that you are overwhelmed, obliterated; you say nothing, because you have lost your voice.

Turn now to those societies where a pre-Gutenberg, pretechnological oral tradition still persists. How do such societies handle their stories, their myths, their poems, their laments, their songs? Do they catechize comprehension—exercise-wise? Do they ask for topic sentences? Not a bit of it: they speak aloud, they sing, they shout, they chant, they whisper, they bellow, they croon, they enact, they dance.

Overwhelming obliteration, Agee would have it, and oral transmission without benefit of pedagogy. Now what do we do with literature? We do what our alter ego insists: and our alter ego may well be a composite introjection of our grade school teacher, our high school teacher, and our college professor. And what did *they* do? They extracted morals—usually prudential, they drilled us in figures of speech or genre theory, and above all they convinced us that literature was something to be done, to be worked on cerebrally, intellectually. And there are established routines, habitual sequences, whereby the task is only performed. And the inappropriateness of the methods is only matched by the inappropriateness of the texts. Ten years ago, I asked the editor in chief of the children's department of the Oxford University Press why, in Britain, they published so few children's novels about living in slums, being in the C stream, having an unemployed father. Her answer came right out of the 19th century parsonage: "We publish books for willing readers". By definition, willing readers are middle class. But in this matter you are doing a much better job than we are: in Britain novels about inner-city kids are patronizing and phony, and poetry about *their* sacred objects hardly exists. But here, in the United States, you—or should I say, the publishers—have a much more urgent sense of what is needed: and many of your best contemporary writers are from the slums. In Britain, the transition from slum dweller to author is very rarely accomplished. So you do have texts in which kids can begin to recognize themselves. One of my favorite pupils in Nebraska—Sidney, a black boy of 12— took a book home for the first time in his life last semester: next morning he was bleary-eyed. "Too much TV last night?" I asked. "No we was reading this book". His fourteen-year-old sister and he had sat up till two o'clock reading to page 115 of the *Collected Poems of Langston Hughes*.

Your *real* books are good—real, that is, as opposed to school-books. (No child would want to sit up till two in the morning reading Roberts: and I want, in all seriousness, to propose that as a criterion for adoption committees.) And some of your schoolbooks are becoming less unreal: I'm thinking especially of the Holt Impact Series. The teacher can stop teaching and leave the book to do the work. Holt has shown that it is possible to produce books that are usually beautiful and startling, textually fascinating, entertaining, and demanding in the right way. And the result of their intelligence and sensitivity is that I, for one, leaving these books around the room, find twelve-year-olds coming up to me—kids not predisposed to pick up books—and saying, "Hey, have you seen this? Did you read that? Man, this sure is a real cool book."

So, in small limited tentative ways, the situation is improving. We are learning to expose kids to books, to make them available in generous quantities, in the classroom where the action is and not in that bleak mausoleum called the school library. We are learning to use paperbacks, and these books are beginning to be stuffed into kids' pockets and read whenever the mood, the desire, or the opportunity arises.

And we are learning that drama is drama and not textual analysis or plotting schemata or character systematization. And we are learning that the kids themselves bring with them so much. Improvisation relates interestingly and fruitfully to other exercises of the mind and of the imagination: it is directed toward the goal of realization, of making real, of making an authentic representation of the world to someone else. It involves control, self-discipline, a focussing of the whole mind and body, an intensity of attentiveness that kids find both deeply absorbing and exhilarating. And within the context of such work a great deal of intensive linguistic activity is taking place, but the attention is not on the language but on the referent, on that which is communicated.

And my quarrel with all the curriculums thus far produced which include elements of linguistics or grammar is precisely this: that by some weird irony they miss precisely those aspects of language which most engage the interest of kids—swearing, joking, riddling, punning, problem posing, playing games with words, slang, creating private languages like Double Fouble or Arjy Parjy, taboos, jive talk, soul talk, insults, technocratic jargon, and so on—in brief, those aspects of language which are instrumental in the kids' business of relating in some way to others or in the organization, the control, the description, or the sharpening of those relationships. Instead, the courses are much concerned with structures, not the dynamic structures of the ways in which we control our relationships, but the structures of sentence patterns. And note this: for every minute that our pupils are working through their textbook exercises, for every such minute they are not assimilating the rich linguistic repertoires of fiction or of poetry: *that* is a serious deprivation.

My final point is this. The English teachers in high schools and the polymaths of the elementary schools, of whom I count myself one, we have not enjoyed a good professional relationship with the high priests in the universities. Astonishingly, the powers that be decided that we were either not mature enough or clever enough to work out our own salvation. But the professors of English or of education, they could do it for us, even though they had not spent more than forty-five consecutive minutes with a class of kids since they themselves left school. So, many of the curriculums—and I don't need to name them—bear the mark of the university imprint:

and it's the wrong imprint. It has all the sequentiality, all the sequaciousness, all the rigorously plotted structures, of a body of knowledge. And it is characterized by a deep ignorance of what makes kids tick, of what switches them on. And such a situation—ineffectively disguised by the ostensible egalitarianism of the curriculum development centers where school teachers are allowed to share a table with the university professors—such a situation is professionally absurd, preposterous, and calamitous.

"After Dartmouth?" A good few years of boredom, of irrelevance, of dry-as-dust academicism, I'd say. I wish I didn't have to say it. And I wish the textbook publishers had to work with the kids for five days a week and live with the consequences of their texts. And above all I wish that NCTE would do something to help the teachers in the schools to do *their* thing and not somebody else's. Is that too much to hope for in a society where you don't have any intellectual authority until you've spent ten of the best years of your life grubbing around for a PhD?

Points for Discussion

1. In what ways is English teaching failing?

   To the English it appeared that our phrase, "Transmitting the cultural heritage," was a deftly concealed euphemism for freezing into the educational system a whole set of middle class values and mores sadly in need of change. (Marckwardt)

   No school system can survive the endless boredom of a curriculum that lacks relevance. (Simpkins)

   In essence, the area between the concreteness of life in the ghetto and the abstractness and meaninglessness of the curriculum has to be bridged if the school is to become a functional part of the student's life. (Minor)

   In short, our curriculum has much to do with students tuning out and dropping out. (Kelly)

   As time wore on I developed less and less respect for content that was there only for reasons of respectability or tradition. (Wilhelms)

   English as we have known it is, I believe, essentially a failure, so bad an investment that it should probably be permitted to wither away. (Wilhelms)

   For many of our children education has little realised relevance; home is relevant; work is relevant; but in the complex of home/school/work it is school that is out of step. (Martin)

2. What should the primary goals of the English program be?

Despite these differences, and they were by no means trivial, the exciting thing that did emerge from the conference was the concept of English as consisting principally of experience and involvement. (Marckwardt)

. . . our job, professionally, is to set up situations in our classrooms which will foster or promote "the active, energetic, cultivated employment of our human endowments." (Summerfield, "Creativity")

3. What is literature for today? How should it be approached?

It is imperative that students and teachers in school situations with no "social problems" become aware of and study the literature and cultural heritage of blacks and other minority groups. (Minor)

I believe we lost our way when we forgot what literature is for. (Wilhelms)

It is not enough for young people to read and study Shakespeare. What is more important is how they feel about Shakespeare after the reading has been completed. (Squire)

Research has amply demonstrated that some of our most able readers, at least those with high scores on standardized reading tests, can be among our most disabled responders. (Squire)

Schools are doing much these days to talk about independent study by pupils; yet how much of this independent study has been employed for wide reading in literature? (Squire)

Your *real* books are good—real, that is, as opposed to schoolbooks. (Summerfield, "Responsibilities")

4. Why teach written composition?

One rarely says anything important in the real sense in talk or in writing unless it is something that he feels, that he is truly motivated to express. (Marckwardt)

It was also true that at Dartmouth the British contingent was content to assume a laissez-faire principle with respect to the speech of the pupils—much less so with their writing, though even here there was far greater concern with the sincerity and immediacy of what they wrote than with the style in which they wrote it. (Marckwardt)

The basic theme-writing, report-making bit, with all its artificialities and formal restraints, is essentially maladaptive, sterile but worse than sterile, actually hostile to real communication. (Wilhelms)

This means that in the schools in our sample, the greatest amount of writing was the recapitulation of work done in lessons or derived from textbooks or notes. (Martin)

5. What stance should English teachers take on the teaching of grammar?

In short, nonstandard grammar has its own logic and its own system, and in fact so does each nonstandard dialect, and as logic and as system there is no reason to consider them either better or worse than the logic and system of the prestige dialect. (Marckwardt)

There was a greater consensus as to the value of linguistics as background information for the teacher than as something to be taught directly. (Marckwardt)

To foster linguistic attainments, we have neglected the bedrock fact that linguistic attainment is fostered by employment rather than by analysis. (Summerfield, "Creativity")

6. Besides engaging in curriculum revision and reassessing methods and materials, how can English teachers strengthen their subject area?

Looking particularly at the English program and repeating that collective bargaining is not an end in itself but a means of attaining a measurably higher quality of language arts instruction . . . . (Simpkins)

Like businessmen, industrialists, military officials, and medical authorities, teachers must learn to spell out in advance the kinds of technological innovations they are seeking. (Simpkins)

7. Where do the greatest challenges lie?

By its very nature, its complexities, its educational, social, and economic needs, the inner city is ripe as a base for creative, imaginative teaching and learning. (Minor)

8. Who or what are English teachers teaching?

And the school system that has a low level of expectation of its socially and economically poor students, that writes them off as dropouts, is passing judgment not on the students but on itself: so when we say of a student as he is about to leave school: "He never did anything worthwhile", we are describing our own failure, the failure of the system, the self-fulfilling prophecies that we have visited on that student more or less from the beginning of his school life. (Summerfield, "Creativity")

. . . all human beings are creative when allowed or encouraged to be so. (Summerfield, "Creativity")

This general behavior pattern suggests that teachers do not want to know their students. It even raises the question of whether teachers want to provide the time or the opportunity for students to truly get to know themselves. (Kelly)

The fundamental question is this: does what we press on a youngster to learn have a reasonable probability of functioning? Will it change his life in desirable ways? Will it change his society in desirable ways? (Wilhelms)

I believe it is imperative that schools dedicate a sizable block of time—say about one-fourth of the day—to a deliberate attempt to help each young person in his personal becoming. (Wilhelms)

Perhaps one of the reasons why we have failed to educate a nation of book readers is that we are so reluctant to give them the opportunity to develop personal reading habits of their own. (Squire)

9. Who are the teachers? What are they saying and doing?

Conveniently, we exempt ourselves—with a rapidity that suggests its source is instinctual—from those teachers whose work practices are right now being called irrelevant or superficial or racist. (Kelly)

Most teachers have never questioned the legitimacy of the power base they straddle as they tower in sometimes dictatorial fashion over their students. (Kelly)

I suggest that we need to know in detail what the language that children encounter in the classroom is like and how the encounters with their teacher's language assist or hinder their learning. (Martin)

We know little enough of the psycho-pathology of teaching—God knows, we need to know much more—but I'd hazard the guess that the textbook-based courses are more generally used by teachers without vivacity, without natural zest and gaiety, without lively, ironic humour: teachers who need the reassurance of Holy Writ, who are themselves insecure in their judgment, and who probably derive much stress from anal compulsions which many of our schools have institutionalized. (Summerfield, "Responsibilities")

Roster of Speakers on Four Major Topics

Benjamin DeMott
Amherst College

David A. Goslin
Russell Sage Foundation

Robert F. Hogan
National Council of Teachers
  of English

Ernece B. Kelly
Chicago City College, Loop Campus

Albert H. Marckwardt
Princeton University

Nancy Martin
University of London
Institute of Education

Sr. Mary Clare, R.S.M.
Mercy High School
Farmington, Michigan

John C. Maxwell
Upper Midwest Regional
  Educational Laboratory

Delores Minor
Detroit Public Schools

William See
Jefferson High School
Portland, Oregon

James R. Squire
Ginn and Company

Edward Simpkins
Harvard University

Geoffrey Summerfield
University of York

Gladys Veidemanis
Oshkosh High School
Oshkosh, Wisconsin

Donald F. Weise
Trenton High School
Trenton, Michigan

Fred T. Wilhelms
Association for Supervision
  and Curriculum Development